.

Verily I say unto you, Except ye be converted, and become as
little children, ye shall not enter into the kingdom of heaven
Matthew, 18.3

Hell is other people.
Jean-Paul Sartre
Hell is thinking there are other people.
Bryan Hubbard

About the author

Bryan Hubbard is a graduate of philosophy from London University.
He is the husband of Lynne McTaggart, author of *The Field*, *The Intention Experiment* and *The Bond*, and together they are directors of their two publishing companies, WDDTY Publishing Ltd and New Age Publishing Ltd.
He is a contributor to, and publisher of, *What Doctors Don't Tell You*, a monthly journal. Previously he has been employed by EMAP and the Financial Times Group.
He lives and works in London with Lynne and their two daughters.

TIME-LIGHT

How your past keeps creating patterns and
problems – and how you can fix it

Bryan Hubbard

New Age Publishing Ltd.

NEW AGE PUBLISHING

Published by New Age Publishing Ltd.
New Age Publishing Ltd., Unit 10 Woodman Works, 204 Durnsford Road, London SW19 8DR

First published by New Age Publishing Ltd 2011

Printed in Great Britain

ISBN: 978-0-9568980-0-5

For Lynne, who lights up my time

CONTENTS

Author's **note**

Every one of us is in thrall to our past, yet few of us realize this, or that we are also on a path to rediscover our true nature. I have written this book for all of you whose quest has become conscious. If you are – or have been – depressed or addicted, and that happens to many travelers along the way, I have some unique insights for you.

You might categorize your quest as personal growth or you see yourself being on a religious or spiritual path; you may believe the goal is enlightenment or nirvana. Whatever you call the journey and the destination, this book is for you. Many of the ideas you will discover in this book offer a new slant on areas of philosophy and spiritually that may seem familiar. I genuinely believe that *Time-Light* offers a unique and insightful understanding of the world's religions and spiritual masters.

How the ideas came to me is not so easy to explain. They seemed to present themselves ready formed, and in the twinkle of an eye. After that, it took me several years to assimilate and think through this instantaneous download, but this process merely added shading to what was already a complete outline.

Some of the exercises in the final part of the book tread on the peripheries of therapies such as Cognitive Behavioural Therapy (CBT) and Gestalt, and on some of the theories of Cybernetics, too. G. I. Gurdjieff also touches on some aspects of my theory in his arcane cosmology. No doubt, eagle-eyed readers will tell me of others.

I had no knowledge of CBT, Gestalt or Cybernetics beyond knowing their names until I started doing some background research for this book; at first, these discoveries gave me comfort that others had had similar thoughts along the way, but I was also concerned that I might be accused of merely copying the thoughts and ideas of others. This is not the case, and the vast majority of the book contains ideas and exercises that you will not have seen anywhere else.

However, there are plenty of people I do acknowledge. I thank Jo Evans for helping to edit the manuscript, and the designer John Clement for his great cover ideas and typography. I thank my two children, Caitlin and Anya, for their help and encouragement, even though they didn't know they were proffering it. Finally, I acknowledge my life-long debt to my wife and soulmate, Lynne McTaggart, who has helped me on every stage of this process, both on and off the page.

Overall, I truly hope and humbly trust that this is an important contribution to our understanding of who we are and our purpose here on Earth.

The Essential **Points**

The Golden Rule: That to which you do not fully attend will weigh you down.

● You are made up of Three Selves, or centers: the Present time-body, the Past time-body and the Potential center.

● The Present time-body includes your body, your brain and the world. The Present time-body also superimposes time and space on the eternal and infinite.

● The Past time-body is itself made up of three sub-centers, or memory types: Knowledge, Narrative and Psychological.

● The Potential center is the unified field of all possibilities.

● The Psychological past is an energetic entity of past hurts and experiences that began to build when you were a small child. It builds from experiences that have not been fully witnessed. In other words, it has been experienced from a partial viewpoint – yours – without taking into account the full circumstances, including the other participants and the causal chains leading to the event. Over time, they build a sense of a substantial self that lessens the sense of unity with the world that you experienced as a child. As time builds in you, so does a sense of space, which separates you from a direct experience with the world.

● Each center is energetic and sends out pulses or waves. The dominant pulse determines who you are at any one time. These pulses are given life by thoughts, emotions and concepts, which are activated in the brain in the Present time-body.

● These pulses are an attempt to find final resolution in the Present. They end when there is complete understanding or a letting go, which happens only with true forgiveness. True forgiveness is seeing the situation itself – the players and the circumstance – and this happens only when all three time-bodies coordinate.

● These pulses create patterns in the Present time-body that become your reality, which is why we often repeat situations from the past.

● As you age, so you become time-heavy as the pulses from the Past time-body increase. You become overwhelmed by life, and you lose sight of any sense of joy or unity. This is because the Past pulses dominate, and they drown out the pulses from the Potential. It manifests as mood swings, irritability, occasional bouts of depression, anxiety and a general sense of anguish.

● A time-heavy person also develops addictions – mild or life-threatening – as the past continues to repeat. A child, by comparison, is *Time-Light*, and his or her pulses primarily come from the Potential center or the Present time-body.

● The way to rediscover your natural state of happiness and sense of unity is first by understanding that you have three centers, and then by becoming conscious of the pulses that primarily emanate from the Psychological past time-body.

● You can achieve this by following the 21-day *Time-Light* program (see Part III).

Foreword

The first thing I noticed about Bryan was his laugh. I was a fellow editor in the shabby offices of a British publishing company in 1985 and, newly separated at the time from a three-year-old marriage, had very little to smile about.

We'd been in the middle of an otherwise uneventful corporate meeting of all the company's editorial and advertising staff when the proceedings were interrupted by an outburst from one corner of the room. One entire editorial team was convulsed in giggles, led by the editor, the loudest of the group.

This was no ordinary laugh. This deep baritone cracked open the silence, seeped into every corner and rained down on every person seated in the room. Indeed, as I discovered when I heard it again in subsequent weeks, Bryan's laugh was fully capable of traversing walls. Although it soon had every one in the room laughing along – a particularly dour group ordinarily – these were not simply copycat gestures. They represented the shock of recognition that occurs when the listener is rare witness to joy emerging straight from the soul.

The resonance of that laugh was all the more astonishing to me after I got to know Bryan in subsequent months and learned something of his history. As a child Bryan had been a victim of child abuse – not physical abuse but mental cruelty of the most potentially debilitating kind. Bryan's father George, an intelligent, if emotionally arrested man, had been severely disappointed in his own life and consequently vented most of his frustration for his life's own shortcomings on his young son, usually in the form of a venomous sarcasm. Bryan had been his father's unwanted third child from a second marriage – and a constant reminder of his own failure to create a loving relationship, particularly with his first wife, who preferred to have her two children taken away from her rather than live with George for one more day.

George refused to acknowledge his son by name and never missed an opportunity to belittle, shout at, or in some way verbally abuse him. Although Bryan was extremely intelligent, his father placed in him a school for tough delinquents, where Bryan essentially survived only by nimble verbal sleight of hand.

George wasn't content to ignore his youngest son's prodigious gifts but did his best to crush them, ignoring a letter from Bryan's school recommending that he apply to Oxford University, so that he was made to leave school at 16. Bryan's mother Edie adored him, but as an orphan who'd never had any parental figures in her own life, and as George's other target, she'd had no blueprint for how to become an encouraging parent. In a sense, Bryan had to grow up and launch his subsequent career as a successful journalist, publisher and entrepreneur in spite of his parents. Often in such a desolate landscape, humor becomes a sanctuary – as does deep spiritual inquiry.

Bryan became a spiritual seeker during his early teenage years, and it was no accident that when he put himself through university as an adult, he pursued a degree in philosophy.

From my perspective, this backstory did not accord in any way with the happy, sensitive person in front of me and the exemplary father he became to our two daughters – except at certain moments. Over the years of our joyful twenty-five year partnership I have observed as Bryan's past occasionally hovers over him like an unwelcome phantom.

In response to some stimulus – a slightly raised voice or the mildest of challenges – he'd angrily lash out. I was stunned by the outsize response until I realized what was going on. He wasn't having a conversation with me. He was still talking to George. He was, as he would now put it, Time-Heavy, trying to put to rest something unresolved from his past.

Over time, I observed this phantom making an appearance with less and less frequency. Bryan preferred mapping the journey to his own understanding and healing rather than taking the ride with a therapist, and like most creative people, he sought to universalize his experience so that ultimately he could help others as well as himself.

As he observed the process of shedding his own phantoms, he began to consider the possibility that the past exists as a separate self in all of us – and becomes, in most cases, the bully of the other selves.

One day, when I returned from a trip, his theory of *Time-Light* and the three selves emerged, fully formed, as if pulled out of thin air, and Bryan then spent many months refining it. Although there are certain parallels with other disciplines, I have yet to find another model that answers so much about the complexity of the human experience with such simplicity.

Other theories that attempt to define consciousness fall short because they do not encompass the intricacies of our lives and the full range of human potential. The majority of programs promising enlightenment fail precisely because they do not take into account the subversive power of the past.

Besides examining the largely negative effect of the past self and how it becomes like a permanent unwanted guest, the *Time-Light* model also provides a brilliant answer to so many of the big questions man has never had adequate answers for – from events that take place "outside of time," such as remote viewing or near death experiences, to human consciousness and its "life" outside of the physical body. As such, the *Time-Light* theory resonates perfectly with my own work on *The Field*, *The Bond* and the power of consciousness.

In addition to laying out one of the most plausible theories I've ever read about what it means to be human, *Time-Light* arms the reader with a powerful set of tools. The step-by-step twenty-one-day program is a comprehensive guide to shedding the burdens of the past and becoming *Time-Light* – and so free, as Bryan puts it, "to fall back in love with your life."

Time-Light resonates so deeply because it speaks with the authentic truth of personal experience. Ultimately, this book represents Bryan's journey, from the pain and darkness of unexamined adversity to understanding and recovered wholeness. May you take to the road with him and learn to travel light.

Lynne McTaggart
March 2011

Introduction

We are never living, but only hoping to live; and looking forward
always to being happy, it is inevitable that we never are so.

Blaise Pascal

What are you aware of right now? This book – or its electronic form – in your hands and the way it feels, of course. The words on the page or screen. Perhaps there is coffee brewing in the other room, and you can smell the aroma. Maybe a car is passing by outside and you can hear it approach, then recede. Your air conditioning system could be whirring away quietly in the background, and you acknowledge that. Whatever is going on right now is the only reality. It has to be – *the here and now is your most real experience*. It can't be the business meeting you had yesterday, or the shopping you did this morning. Although they happened, the reality of those experiences has diminished and been replaced by this moment, with this book in your hands.

While that is obvious, we don't live as though it is. For most of us, the business meeting or the argument with our spouse is living on right now, and may even be making it difficult to concentrate on the words in front of you. Are you present enough to understand the words that you are reading?

As we get older, and have more experiences, the here and now becomes less apparent. We become *time-heavy*. The mess we make of our life demonstrates this. We fall out of love, we divorce, we struggle with money, we take antidepressants, drugs or alcohol or all three; we get stuck in jobs we can't stand, we have children we can't communicate with any more, we spend hours watching TV programs we don't like, and finally, when we collapse exhausted into our bed, we don't sleep. For the rest of the time we have mood swings, we get irritable, and we suffer bouts of depression and despondency. It's as though we have been possessed by an entity over which we have almost no control.

I'm going to show you how your past makes up your reality, and why you will continue to relive your experiences until you understand that you are living life on permanent repeat. The most common symptom of this recurring past is depression, anxiety and a sense of pointlessness. Its most common manifestation is a pattern of addictions.

The understanding of this past-to-present movement – and of you in and through time – is the golden thread that we will follow. Once you have exorcised the ghosts of your past – and this book will show you how to do this day by day – you will begin to live fully and joyfully in the present. You will also feel "at one" with the world, and the sense of separation and isolation that you have will vanish.

The law of distraction
Thoughts help to shape our reality and us – it's an idea that is hardly news. The major religions touch on this truth, as do thinkers in the New Age movement, who call the phenomenon anything from the Law of Attraction to The Secret and manifestation.

Although the New Age philosophy is simplistic, it is nonetheless true that we repeat patterns in our life. An abused wife will often choose a second husband who also abuses her, business owners with money problems continue to make the same mistakes again in subsequent businesses, and people who are suspicious of others rarely make friends. Married couples whose own parents divorced are themselves more likely to break up. Children who were abused in any way – even if the abuse is no more than being shouted at once in a while – are more likely to suffer chronic disease as an adult, and even die prematurely.

Patterns don't just appear in a lifetime – they also seem to settle through the generations like sedimentary layers. Sociologists have noted that a tendency to commit suicide runs through families, and parents whose own parents were alcoholics often are themselves addicts or have children who become addicts. Similarly, those who were raised in a household afflicted by a parent with gambling problems will also display similar traits – or, again, their children will. The reality of the past will create the circumstances in their lives right now and will continue to do so until they wake up to the unconscious processes that are wrecking their lives and those of their children.

We can all recognize these patterns, whether their origins are from our own experiences or from a *leitmotif* of a family or close community, even if few of us have completely understood how they happen. Biologists maintain that behaviorial patterns are the result of genetics and the imprinting in our DNA, but the science of epigenetics – which studies outside influences on DNA coding – tells us that our environment, including the people in it, are more powerful influences and can overwrite genetic coding. In other words, the sciences aren't entirely sure what's going on here.

It is a law of attraction in one sense, but actually a law of distraction as these patterns lead us away from a happy and rich life, which can be lived only in the present moment.

The Greeks had a word for it
Many of us also have a sense of separation – from the world, our family and even our own body. This feeling of isolation grows as we age, until we begin to see ourselves as utterly alienated from

the world. Along the way, our inability to connect has a high price: in divorce, in children who drift into alcohol and drug abuse, and in depression or heart disease, both classic symptoms of isolation. If you are one of the few who does not suffer from some kind of depression, you may instead have addictions.

Although you start life as a child who felt at home in the world, you become an adult who feels separate, as though you are looking through a large pane of frosted glass, cut off from a direct experience of living.

This nightmarish transformation of a world that once felt like home to one that is alien and even hostile has been recognized through the millennia. The Ancient Greeks described this sense of disconnectedness as *anguish*, and it perfectly describes the feeling of separation that grows in us until it eventually wrings the joy from our lives.

Who am I?

So what then is happening? Why do patterns recur in your life, and why do you feel increasingly separated from the world? Why has life ceased to be joyful, and instead you feel flat, irritable, depressed even, and suffer mood swings? To understand that, we must first unlock one of the oldest metaphysical puzzles: who am I, the central player in the drama? Unless we are able to answer this question, and see who this "I" is and its relationship to the world and time, we cannot fully understand how it is that the past has us so much in its thrall and why we feel disconnected and unhappy with our life.

Most of us go through life without ever thinking about what the "I" is. Somehow, we just think that "I" is a substantial, conscious entity that sits in our brain, a constant, never-changing self that is always observing or thinking. If we did some self-reflection, we would probably concur with the current paradigm that the idea of "I" arises from the body. If we are religious, we might instead think this "I" is our soul, which will survive our death and live on in Heaven or reincarnate into another body.

Although we think of ourselves as one complete and coherent entity that we refer to as "I", we ignore the conflicts that often occur within us. If we are just a body, what is it in us that decides to commit suicide or why do we sacrifice ourselves to a higher good? Why do we say one thing, but believe another? Why do we contradict ourselves or constantly change our mind? Why do we become addicted to alcohol, cigarettes or a drug when we know we are probably killing ourselves? These actions suggest that there is more than one thing going on to make you a "you".

The first clue

I finally started to realize what we really are when I was presented with two clues, years apart. The first happened with the death of my father. He was in his ninetieth year, and yet there was absolutely nothing wrong with him physically. A check-up a few years previously had revealed that he had the heart of someone twenty or thirty years younger. Yet, there he was, on the day I went to see him at his home, lying in bed.

"What's wrong?" I asked.

Nothing much, he replied with a shrug, other than that he had had enough. He had become tired of life, and now he wanted to die, he said. He turned away from me and faced the wall.

Hours later, as I was leaving, I put my head around the bedroom door and gave a tentative goodbye. I had the fleeting thought that it would be the last time I would see him, even though the idea seemed absurd. He wished me well, and I left. Three days later my mother telephoned to tell me that my father had died.

In a sense, he had wished his own death. There was no post

mortem, but had there been one, the cause of death probably would have been something general and vague, such as old age, but certainly not "tired of life," or "had enough," or even "couldn't stand another day of this."

If you are lucky, you will die of old age. Doctors, family and friends will all agree that you had a good life. Medicine does not recognize old age as a cause of death, even though every day somebody seems to die from it. Certainly, your body gets "worn out," or you lose the zest for life. You will have seen much and, like my father, you will have felt the enormous weight of past regrets, disappointments and hurts that you are carrying around. As the English poet William Wordsworth put it, "The world is too much with us."

On the day I visited my father, he was both a body that was talking to me in the bedroom in present time, and a past that seemed to inhabit him. In the end, that's what happens to most of us – the past bears down on us, as if it were a separate being, until we can't stand it, not even for one more day.

The second clue

The other clue came to me years later, when I read a book about ghosts. My wife, Lynne McTaggart, was abroad, lecturing somewhere, my eldest daughter was at her university, and my youngest was with friends. That left me with our pet dog, Ollie, and a shelf of books that I wanted to read. However, nothing I brought out into the garden seemed to hold my interest, so I wandered back into the house, and into Lynne's study, which is lined with books that she uses for her research. I don't know why, but one book caught my attention. It was called *Visions of Immortality* (Element, 1998) by Ian Currie, a Canadian university professor who had carried out a thorough review of the evidence for life after death, ghosts and apparitions. Perhaps it was the title, which reminded me of a Wordsworth poem, or that it "called me", as some books do to us, but whatever the reason, I took it from the shelf and back to my seat in the garden.

Up until then, I had had almost no interest in ghosts. I had assumed they were either the creations of a fevered imagination or the inventions of attention-seekers. I was astonished by what I read, and my preconceptions were turned on their head.

Currie had documented tale after tale of ghost stories or, more precisely, instances of contact with those who had died. The stories were highly plausible, the people who related them had far more to lose than gain from the telling, and they were all independently verifiable. Currie demonstrated, beyond any reasonable doubt, that something of us survives death. But what is it? It seemed to be something that still had unfinished business on earth – invariably a message that had to be delivered through an emotionally-charged entity. It was not physical – clearly not, as the body had died – and so it must be energetic. However, there is nothing extraordinary in that: physics tells us that everything ultimately is energy. Seen that way, it is reasonable to consider that our body and this "ghost" that survives death are expressions of two different forms of energy.

Here was another demonstration that the past has an independent existence as a separate body of experiences, upsets, sadness, and possibly even trauma. It haunts us while we live, and eventually it kills us. According to Currie, it even lives on after we die. Whether or not you believe in ghosts, it is a potent metaphor for a past that seems to be another "me" that lives in my body. The past is not just a collection of memories, but a palpable and energetic force that creates patterns in your life.

The past inside us
The past can also have a psychosomatic effect. How many

times have you felt your stomach knot up as you think about someone who has upset you? Does an event in the past still have the power to make you angry today? As you will read later on, bad things that happen to us as children can make us chronically ill when we are adults. The event doesn't have to be as severe as sexual molestation; it can be anything from a father who shouts at us, to a mother who is never at home when we come back from school. Even though the parents may be dead, their power is such that they can reach out through time and give us a fatal heart attack. How could that happen, unless the past lives on in us as some energetic entity? If that entity can survive independently of physical time – and hurts live on irrespective of the existence of the perpetrator – then Currie's idea that they survive beyond the death of the physical body is not such a huge step to take after all.

As the past grows, so we feel increasingly separate from the world. Our sense of a self – made up of past sufferings, sadness, regrets and disappointments – becomes a fortress against a world that is hostile and against us. As the past grows in us, so does a sense of space that separates us from the world.

So what are you that you can live in the present and yet be more influenced by the past, which separates you from the world? *You are a time machine*: you create an imagined future from a past that you did not completely understand in the first place. This continual time projection – from past to future – bypasses the present, and events in the present moment are invariably seen and interpreted through the filter of the past. As a result, you never fully experience the moment, when any seeming division between you and the world would evaporate and the fortress walls of the self melt.

As a self that is made up of the past, you are a complex mass of feelings and emotions that strike out at any moment, like a volcano that is always ready to blow. The trouble is that you don't know what may trigger your outburst. It could be the wrong word at the wrong time, a situation you encounter, even a toothpaste tube squeezed the wrong way.

You don't do it because you are a "bad" person. Having angry outbursts or occasional emotional eruptions isn't an aspect of your inherent nature – it happens because you truly want to understand. This book will explain why that is, why we feel hurt and upset in the first place, where these feelings of hurt come from and what the whole process is trying to achieve. As you read this book, you will start to recognize an energetic impulse that seeks understanding through you as a body in time and space. While you are unaware of this movement, you are living unconsciously. You are often unconscious of the referencing, the projection from the past into a future. Yet it colors your world every moment, and the more you are in the thrall of these waves of psychological time, the less happy you are.

Most thoughts and feelings have their origins in the past. These feelings are the accumulation of hurts, disappointments and upsets that happened some time in the past. That past may be just a few seconds old, as happens when we think about solving a problem that has just cropped up, but it is more often from years ago.

The past becomes a weight, as it did for my father and as it does for many of us. Yet how does this affliction of time happen? How did we become time machines in the first place?

Your Three Selves

If the past is a "body" or energy center, and if you already have a physical body, this suggests you have more than one body. Indeed, you have, and here we get to the engine room of *Time-Light*. But you do not have just two bodies or selves – you have three. You may live in present time, while being more influenced by the past, but you also have experiences that seem to be outside of space and time. These strange phenomena – the intuitive leap, the sense you just "knew" something was going to happen, or the dream that foretells a future event – suggest that there is a third "you" that is not dependent on time.

I call the selves, or centers, the Present time-body, the Past time-body and the Potential center. It might seem an extraordinary thought that you are the amalgam of three entities, each calling itself "me" or "I," but this is not so alien a concept if you are from the Christian tradition. One of the axioms of Christianity is the idea of the three-in-one God: the Father, Son and Holy Ghost. But Jesus' teachings were distorted. His original doctrine, espoused in the Gospels, stated that God is within us. Yet, within years of the establishment of the Christian Church, this radical idea was replaced by one that situated God in a distant Heaven, reached primarily through the intercessory powers of the priests.

The notion that we are made up of Three Selves is also not such a surprise to those of you immersed in ancient philosophy, especially that of Plato, who told us we were a blend of the intellect, passions and spirit.

The three-in-one self is the basis of Freudian psychology, which proposes that we are made up of an ego, a subconscious and an unconscious, and the ancient wisdom schools often refer to the three bodies of the self – the gross body of the physical world, the subtle body of feelings and images, and the causal body of subtle energy.

So what is so special about the *Time-Light* model? It is one of the first to explore who we are in and through time, a dimension that I believe is the key to our understanding. From this understanding we can achieve fulfilment, creativity and joy. *Only when we clearly see ourselves as a creation of time and the past can we begin to live fully in the present moment – and lose our sense of separation, alienation and anguish.*

Of the Three Selves in my model, the Past time-body causes most of our worries and, indeed, most of the strife in the world. It is the seat of both depression and addictions — as such, they have the same origins. It is where the past accumulates and the past-to-future movement occurs. As we grow older, the Past time-body has more energy from experiences and so becomes more substantial. By the time we reach adulthood, we have become time-heavy. We are more past than present, whereas, when we are small children, we are *Time-Light*, more in the present moment than in the past. My father had become so time-heavy that life became too much, and he wanted it to end.

Do you remember when you were a small child, when you were *Time-Light*? You probably have some memories of that time, and they were likely to be idyllic (unless you were in an abusive family). Moments seemed to go on forever, and the slightest thing could fascinate you for hours. You felt at one with the world. It was your home, your playground, and any division between you and that world was slight. If you have small children yourself, their wonder at the world should remind you of how it is to be *Time-Light*

Is that how you live your life every day now? I doubt it. Instead, it is likely that commitments and worries weigh you down, you are always planning for some imagined future, and you are concerned about money, your job, your family and children. It is natural to ensure you are secure, that you have enough food, proper shelter, and that you have good health — but is this supposed to take the joy out of your life?

Life for you today is invariably mundane, occasionally a struggle and, in the main, tolerable. You enjoy moments of happiness and joy, and reward yourself with the odd holiday, nice meal, bottle of wine or latest movie. However, beneath this activity lies an undefined sense that life could and should be better, if only you knew how. At this point, some of us get the "spiritual bug" and desire enlightenment, bliss or nirvana, without recognizing that the very desire is merely a movement – from past unhappiness to an imagined joy in the future – that is the exact same as the one that covets the new Mercedes.

The metaphysical itch
Our tragedy is that, deep down, we do know that money or a big new house aren't quite going to hit the spot, that we have been locked out of an unspoken inheritance, a metaphysical right that came with our birth. Material success is a pale imitation of the glory that somehow should be ours. It is a little like the cosmic joke: "Most of us go though life not knowing what we want, but feeling damned sure that this isn't it."

You can get a sense of this by looking at your own life. Many of us live with a general sense of malaise, a greyness or fog that seems to have descended over the sun-filled days of our early childhood, and we suffer anything from frequent irritation and regular angry outbursts to occasional stress, anxiety, phobias, or even chronic depression and finally to suicidal thoughts.

Many of us feature somewhere along this spectrum of desperate living. Life overwhelms one in five of us to such an extent that we regularly take a powerful antidepressant just to get through the day, and some one million people around the world commit suicide every year. Even if we eschew the antidepressant, many of us have various addictions – to alcohol, food, drugs, gambling, cigarettes or even sex.

The central purpose of this book is to renew you and your life, consciously to erase the past that weighs you down, to reconnect you to the world – and to make you *Time-Light*. In order to do so, however, I need to explain various ideas, which I do throughout this book. In summary, I demonstrate:

● "You" are made up of Three Selves, or energy centers.

● Those centers are the Present, the Past and the Potential.

● The Present includes the body and brain, and the world of time and space. Time and space are constructs of the Present time-body.

● The Past is an accumulation of experience. As you grow older, the Past time-body becomes more substantial, and you become time-heavy. The Past time-body begins to dominate. In a *Time-Light* person, usually a child, the Present time-body and the Potential center dominate. A dominant Past time-body also disconnects you from the world and from others.

● The past accumulates when we do not fully witness the experience in the moment. We cannot completely understand any experience if it is seen entirely through our own eyes, and not from the perspective of others as well, or without knowledge of the overall situation. A fully witnessed experience leaves no energetic print in the Past time-body.

● As energy centers, the time bodies send out pulses or waves, which the brain interprets as thoughts and emotions. The dominant pulse from one of the centers determines our sense of self at any given time. This is why you continuously change. The sense of self as a constant fixed point is a fiction.

● These pulses are attempts by the Past time-body in particular to achieve completion and final understanding. Experience happens only in time and space, and the Past seeks to relive experiences that we never completely understood in the first place. It is a hopeless endeavor. The one constant of the Present time-body is change and so, by definition, it is impossible to replicate a situation, as people and circumstances can never again be the same. The Present time-body therefore either creates a similar situation – an abused wife will seek another abuser – or create a mirror pattern, where the drive is towards the very opposite of the actual past experience. The third possible response is the displaced concept, where a situation reminds you of an experience and triggers the full emotional outburst from the previous occasion.

● As time-heavy people, we create more patterns from the past, and we continue to repeat events as the past seeks to understand itself.

● Addictions are also repeat patterns that seek final and complete understanding. They are not from an impulse to forget, nor are they born of sadness – they are energy waves that seek to remember, originating from moments of ecstasy and unity.

● We have neither a subconscious nor an unconscious; instead, we have energy centers that seek resolution. Far from being suppressed, all of our thoughts and feelings, even the most subliminal, are constantly pulsing to the Present time-body, which is the only center in which they can be played out and resolved. The momentum of all the selves is towards greater understanding: the Present endeavors to do so through the sciences and arts, the Past by seeking resolution through a complete comprehension of experience, and the Potential, a unified field, through the creation of time, space and separation, and to understand itself in relationship – ultimately to itself.

Understanding ourselves in and through time is the key to the door to a life that is always in the present and joyful. It is also the essence of most of the world's great religions, and teaching us to become *Time-Light* is their ultimate aim, even if this is not always explicitly stated. Jesus' pivotal teachings concern man in time. He taught us to take no thought of the morrow, and his exhortation to become as little children – which I have made as the key quote at the beginning of this book – is his call for us to become *Time-Light*. He is inviting us to live in the moment, without the weight of the past.

The Buddha said something similar; according to The Dhammapada, he declared, "What we are today comes from our thoughts of yesterday, and our present thoughts build our life of tomorrow: our life is the creation of our mind." In the following verse, the Buddha then states, "He insulted me, he hurts me, he defeated me, he robbed me. Those who think such thoughts will not be free from hate." This statement is an expression of the movement of time through thoughts that create our reality. We think our world into being.

The Hindu Upanishads tell us: "According as a man acts and walks in the path of life, so he becomes. He that does good becomes good; he that does evil becomes evil. By pure actions he becomes pure; by evil actions he becomes evil". All these texts are trying to demonstrate that the key is in understanding the self in and through time, and that this self is entirely a construct of thought. Strangely, the sense of self is the one thing that we never define. Instead, we assume we already know what we are because, after all, what could be closer than our thoughts?

The great religions and the mystics have all tried different messages through the ages to help us unlock the door. We have been told variously to overcome the ego, to transcend ourselves, to be still. Even today, we are reminded of the power of now.

The key to a transcendent life lies in the understanding of the self as both a process of time and outside of time: the power of *how*, if you will. This book, especially the 21-day program at the end, gives you the true meaning and reward of every religion. Ultimately, as you grow into the *Time-Light* method, you might quietly lose the need for the structures of organized religion. Ultimately, no religion, method or philosophy captures your depth and mystery. You will even come to view the *Time-Light* program as a necessary step along the way, but one that you have grown beyond. In its place will be you as a natural being, a *Time-Light* person.

By the end of this book, I hope you will be living completely in the present, a *Time-Light* being who is living life to the fullest, and bringing into the world the full potential you were born to deliver. You will understand that you are part of a unified field, and that you are connected to everything and everyone. Your fate will not be that of my father – and, sadly, millions of others – who are inhabited by a past whose heaviness wore them down until life wasn't worth living.

Part One
You and Time

Chapter 1
You in the now

Inside and outside are inseparable. The world is wholly inside and I am wholly outside myself.
Maurice Merleau-Ponty

An ancient Vedic scripture marveled that although everyone dies, nobody seems to mind. It described the phenomenon as one of the wonders of the world. Indeed it is, because it would be rational for us to fear our death, our absolute destruction, yet few, if any of us, actually do.

Most of us are embroiled in the rush of the daily round, and so we do not have the time or inclination to ponder esoteric musings such as the nature of the self and its relationship to time and space. If we did, we would probably recognize the current scientific model – that the sense of a "me" arises from the fact that there is a body. This body lives through the dimensions of time and space, which are independent of the body, and you have little, if any, influence over them. You and the world, therefore, are separate from each other.

Neuroscience would agree. According to current theory, this sense of a "me", which feels so substantial, is the result of nothing more than a series of complex neural firings between different areas of the brain. Neureoscientists tell us that the human brain is made up of three parts: the old reptilian brain, which is concerned with survival, the mid-brain, which processes emotions, and the new brain, especially the pre-frontal cortex, where language, speech, reading and thinking all happen. This most recent development of the brain makes us human and separates us from the other animals.

Cumulatively, the sense of a substantial "you" is as a ghost in the machine of the body, as philosopher Gilbert Ryle once put it. When the body dies, the brain dies, and, with it, any sense of you. Similarly, if parts of the brain die, so parts of "you" die, too, as we see in Alzheimer's or dementia patients.

If that model is correct, we return to our original Vedic question: why do you not fear your death? As I said, it would be rational to fear one's demise, so it could be because we are irrational. If we are merely neural firings, we do not have the imagination to fear our end, and if time and space are dimensions that are absolute and separate from us we do not have the capacity to grasp such an eventuality.

The Vedic question was, of course, a loaded one. We do not fear our death because "we" do not die, even though every body does die, the Vedas tell us. If every body dies, then you are not the body, and the "real you" cannot be an insubstantial phenomenon that arises from the brain's neural circuitry.

You and the world
The prevailing scientific model tells us that the sense of "you" arises from the body, which is dependent on the ability to receive sensory data from the world. Therefore, we start with a world, then a body in the world, and finally a sense of you that arises from the brain's activities because of sensory data input. With this model, science has created a complete division between object (the world) and subject (you). The human race shall know the world through the rational mind and the sciences, and not through some mystical union with a world that we discern through magic, superstition and tea leaves in the bottom of a cup.

> *Current view of the world and how the sense of a self arises*
>
> WORLD (Time/Space) ➤ BODY ➤ SELF

Although we are capable of amazing thought constructions, it all starts from the raw data from our senses. We wouldn't know, for example, that a hot poker is hot until we touched it, or that lemons have a bitter taste until we tasted one, or that a flower has a scent until we smelled a rose. We also fuse separate pieces of sense data, so we know a rose has thorns and that lemons have a rough skin. By giving names to things in the world, we have constructed a language. From understanding number, space and elevation in space and time, we create a conceptual world of geometry, maths, and equations. Not only that, we can project our sense data into realms that don't even exist, and imagine golden horses or castles made of clouds.

Nevertheless, we cannot imagine the golden horse if we have not already seen a horse and something made of gold. We cannot envision a castle made from clouds if we do not know what both a castle and a cloud look like. Even the mathematician wrestling with the most esoteric equations has to start with a world and sensory input, no matter how far his formulae may take him. There is no such thing as a brain in complete isolation from the world, and this brain thinks and rationalizes because of the sensory data it is constantly receiving.

This all seems like good common sense at first glance, but these supposedly firm foundations start to look a little shaky the deeper we dig. Are we really just a body with some cleverness thrown in? Our emotions and feelings suggest that we are something more. Doctors are beginning to recognize the important role that our emotions play in determining our state of health and our recovery from disease. This emerging science, known as psychoneuroimmunology, already recognizes that stress and emotions play an important role in inflammatory diseases such as arthritis (Psychological Bulletin, 2007; 133: 1007-37) and that our level of self-esteem determines the health of our heart (Personality and Social Psychological Review, 2008; 12: 370-89).

Being happy and not worrying also dramatically reduces our chances of developing chronic heart failure. A study by Columbia University Medical Center in New York, which involved 1,739 participants over a ten-year period, established that our attitudes toward life have a direct and powerful effect on the heart. Happy people who tend not to overly worry about things are far less likely to suffer heart problems than are their more gloomy counterparts (European Heart Journal, 2010; 31: 1065-70).

Women who have suffered recurrent episodes of breast cancer dramatically reduce the risk of a further bout just by learning a few skills to reduce their stress levels. In one experiment involving 227 women with breast cancer, those who were taught how to lower stress had a 45 per cent reduced risk of developing the cancer again, and they were cancer-free even eleven years afterwards (Clinical Cancer Research, 2010; 16: 3270-8). Positive thoughts really do aid wellness, just as negative ones make us ill. Consequently, the idea of the self as a simple sensory-related phenomenon starts to get a little more complicated. Our sense of self in time can be changed by the way we feel.

The world through our senses

And can we entirely rely on our senses? Is my sense of "red" the same as yours? Can we agree on what "hotness" is? To illustrate the point, researchers have carried out experiments with a chemical called phenol-thio-urea. To most people, it has a bitter taste, but for around a quarter of those who have taken part in tasting experiments, it has no taste at all. So is the chemical bitter or not? Putting it another way, is the bitterness in the chemical, or in our senses?

The world we experience through our senses is not the same world that other living things see, hear and taste. Biologists have discovered that bees see a color range beyond our visual capacity, that ants sense polarized light, that bats detect warmth from another living thing up to six inches (sixteen centimeters) away, that cats have a hearing range between 100 and 60,000Hz, and that dolphins hear sounds up to at least 100,000Hz. Our hearing range is a mere 20,000Hz by comparison. The lowest register we hear is at approximately 20Hz, whereas an elephant can hear a sound as low as 1Hz. The humble pig with its 15,000 taste buds can taste things that we cannot detect with our 9,000, and a pig pales in comparison to the rabbit, which has 20,000 taste buds.

Therefore, our senses are not capable of telling us everything about the world that apparently sits outside of us. It has colors, sounds and tastes well beyond our sensual spectrum, yet the world for the bat and the bee is as real for them as ours is for us. So, what is real? Is there an absolute reality?

The new sciences are also blurring the edges that apparently divide you from the world outside of your body. A new branch of biology known as epigenetics is challenging the theory that you are entirely the result of the genetic codes in your DNA. Epigeneticists now believe that our genes are switched on and off by atoms above the gene that are affected by our immediate environment: the food we eat, the pollutants we are exposed to and the level of stress we encounter. Lars Olov Bygren, a specialist in preventive health at the Karolinska Institute in

Stockholm, researched the parish records of a remote town in northern Sweden and discovered evidence of an environmental effect that has passed down through the generations (European Journal of Human Genetics, 2007; 15: 784-70). A famine at key moments in the lives of grandparents directly affected the life expectancy of the grandchildren, irrespective of their genetic profile. Environmental factors have overwritten genetic code.

A similar situation occurred with women who were pregnant at the time of the 9/11 terror attack on the World Trade Center in New York. Psychologist Rachel Yehuda at the Mount Sinai School of Medicine in New York has discovered that women who were either inside the building or close to it at the time when the attack occurred have passed on the effects of their stress at the time to their children (Yehuda, R. *Treating Trauma Survivors with PTSD*, American Psychiatric Publishing Inc, 2002).

Professor Wolf Reik at the Babraham Institute in Cambridge has demonstrated that the switches that control our genetic coding are themselves inherited, suggesting that a "memory" of an event passes through the generations. As he says, genes and the environment are not mutually exclusive, but are inextricably intertwined, with one affecting the other. If you are as much your environment as you are your DNA, where do you actually begin and end?

Darwin's theory of evolution also supports this blurring of the dividing line between body and world, subject and object. Evolutionists may make statements such as, "Dinosaurs evolved into birds" or "The hairy mammoth evolved into today's elephant," but this is not what happened at all. Dinosaurs were not self-willed agents that decided to become birds in order to survive; instead, the environment in

8

particular, and life in general, changed the dinosaur. Those type of lazy statements mask the reality that the environment shapes you as much as your inherited DNA. You are not a set of pre-determined pieces of genetic code on legs; you are also part of a dynamic world, which is as much you as you are it. While Darwin believed this process happens over millions of years, epigeneticists are demonstrating that DNA can be overwritten in a generation.

The cognitive philosopher Alva Noe at the University of California at Berkeley has demonstrated how the environment plays a key role in creating our sense of a self and our interior landscape. Our visual apparatus is a vital way for us to learn about the world around us – but Noe invites us to consider what would happen to someone who, for some reason, was not permitted to see as an infant. Although it is difficult fully to comprehend the difference between the consciousness of someone deprived of sight and someone who has enjoyed full visual stimulation, the inability to see will affect the development of neural interconnections that are necessary for vision. Thus, in some way, the boy deprived of sight during the crucial years when his brain is developing will be different from the boy whose sight was not impaired. The environment, therefore, has affected the boy in Noe's thought experiment and has contributed to making him that which he has become.

Your innate connection with the world
We seem to have an innate knowledge of the world that goes beyond the data fed to us by our senses. If I show you a color chart, with subtle and changing shades, you will be able to detect if a shade is missing from the spectrum, even though you have never seen the chart before. Similarly, if you hear a range of

several octaves, you will know instantly if the musician does not play one of the notes.

Neuroscientists argue that these patterns are hardwired into our brain, but how did this happen and where did the brain get the pattern from in the first place? The immediate answer to the latter question is to suggest that it comes from the world itself, but, of course, the response is circular. If that is the case, how did the brain know there was a missing color or note in order for the evolutionary hardwiring to begin?

There are similar problems about our sense of beauty and morality. While both seem to be subject to change, fashion and social values, there is an essence to both that transcends time. I well remember taking our youngest daughter, when she was eight, to The Louvre in Paris. As we turned a corner, the headless statue of Winged Victory, carved more than two thousand years ago, confronted us. My daughter stopped in her tracks, and looked in utter awe at the sculpture before her. "It's beautiful," she gasped. Of course, it is, and hundreds of generations before us would agree, as, doubtlessly, will the generations that follow us. So what was it in my daughter, more familiar with images of pop stars, that could register beauty in an ancient statue that is missing vital parts?

The same goes for basic right and wrong. While morality changes with societal mores, our fundamental sense of rightness and fairness seems to run like a seam throughout history. Although most mothers have intervened to make their child share with another, researchers have also noticed that a sense of fairness and of taking turns is inherent in one-year-olds. Yet, where does such an abstract idea as rightness and turn-taking come from if we cannot pick it up through our senses? Do we get it from the world, and, if not, what is this mysterious osmosis that happens within months of our birth?

We have an intimate relationship with the world and to the events that happen in time and space. We are at home in the world. We know when the ground in front of us is substantial, and when we reach out for a piece of paper, we are confident that we will be able to touch it. We can even predict events or assess that we cannot cross the road safely because the car is traveling too fast, or know that we can catch the ball if we move a few steps to the right.

If we are ultimately sense-input beings, as the current scientific view suggests we are, there are only limited ways that we get information and knowledge. We can do so through an association of ideas – such as conjuring up that golden horse in our imagination or figuring out an equation – or from matters of fact; we know from experience, for instance, that water is wet. So how is it possible for us to have pre-existing patterns in our head that tell us a color or a note is missing, that give us a universal sense of beauty, an inherent sense of right and wrong, and an ability to predict something we may never have seen before?

You create time and space
We cannot answer these questions without coming up with an answer that takes us on an endless loop. What comes first? Us or the world? If it's us, how can we be affected and shaped by the world? If it is the world, how can we have an innate sense of right and wrong, color and beauty?

One solution – mooted more than two hundred years ago by the philosopher Immanuel Kant, after spending years pondering the very same issues – is that we ourselves impose the framework of time and space onto a canvas that, because it must have neither of those dimensions, is eternal and infinite. It is a brilliant solution, and one that solves the "world knot" as Kant's disciple, Arthur Schopenhauer, described the relationship between us and the world. The answer is that neither the world nor humanity came first, but both are inextricably codependent on the other. Without a body – and a brain that creates the matrix of time and space – there would be no world, and yet, in a symbiotic dance, our body is in the world of its own creation.

Kant was one of the first philosophers to try to explain consciousness, the elusive "thing" that is more than merely a brain activity that allows us to have sensory experiences. As Kant demonstrated, consciousness is the ground of being that encompasses the world and us in a two-way supportive relationship.

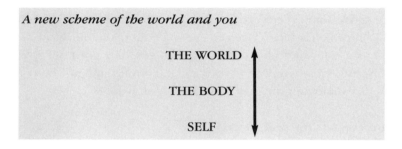

A new scheme of the world and you

THE WORLD

THE BODY

SELF

Kant's revolutionary premise presaged the discoveries of quantum physics some 120 years later. Kant posited our central role in the cocreation of the world in time and space, and quantum physicists have demonstrated that there is no phenomena of "stuff," or reality, until it is observed. In essence, the world comes into being in the very act of observing it.

The eminent quantum physicist Eugene Wigner remarked that consciousness was the only reality: "It was not possible to formulate the laws of quantum mechanics in a fully consistent way without reference to the consciousness of the observer. The very study of the external world led to the conclusion that the content of consciousness is the ultimate reality."

Wigner was one of the figureheads of a new branch of quantum physics that positions perception at the very heart of creation itself, just as Kant had concluded. However, there are paradoxes within the paradox: If Wigner is correct, am I dependent on others for my existence? Do others perceive me into being?

Quantum physics tells us that the phenomena of time and space occur only at the collapse of the wave function, when quantum particles "solidify" into measurable matter. Nevertheless, scientists have argued about where the demarcation line occurs. For Wigner and his followers, it must be at the moment of perception, as we freeze quantum particles into a specific time and space, and we need a continual regress of perception so that you – and me – can exist, a phenomenon he called "Wigner's friend." Wigner's friend perceives Wigner into being, who perceives his friends into being, *ad infinitum*. We are therefore creating and being created at every moment.

Kant, Wigner and others may not have fully appreciated the extent of the paradox. While I perceive the world into being, my body – and my brain, as the perceiving instrument – become part of its own creation. This suggests that the real perceiver is not my brain, or my body at all, which, in turn, means that I am not my body, but ultimately that which sees my body into being.

No wonder we do not fear our death.

Summary: The prevailing view that the sense of an "I" is created from the outside in – from the world, to a body, to a sense of you – rests on a circular argument in order to explain the special relationship we have with the world and how we know things beyond our sensory data. We can explain that special relationship – and get rid of the circularity – only if we see ourselves as cocreators of the world we inhabit, imposing time and space onto a canvas that is eternal and infinite. We not only live in the present, we also create it. This special relationship dissolves the dividing line between my body and the

world. I also influence the world around me through my thoughts and my feelings. Reality is not just something that happens to me; it is something that I cocreate.

Chapter **2**
You and the past

There is no present or future, only the past, happening over and over again, now.
Eugene O'Neill, A Moon for the Misbegotten

Every moment we are experiencing. We experience the sensation of the chair under our legs, the hum of the air-conditioning system, the taste of the coffee we have just drunk. These are primarily neutral experiences and they form the backdrop of our life. Most of these experiences pass through us, so to speak, and they make up the sensory data that tell us there is a world out there and that we are having an experience in it.

However, not all experiences are quite so neutral. Some go beyond pure sensory input and require your involvement as a being that thinks and feels. You might meet an acquaintance in the street – so how do you respond? Almost inevitably, the past plays a part. If you know the person you unexpectedly bump into, it would seem strange and very anti-social to walk past without acknowledging him or her. The meeting will also produce some quick shorthand about the person – even if you are not immediately conscious of it – telling you if the person is to be welcomed or avoided. The same goes for a problem you may need to solve. You will call on your experience and any training and expertise you have in order to resolve it.

These are examples of when memory is a friend – when it helps you to navigate your way around the world. However, memory can also be less coherent or clear. Sometimes it is like a quick movement that you just glimpse out of the corner of your eye. This is the memory of past events and experiences, not always fully recalled, but that nonetheless has an energetic charge. Often these memories are associated with a feeling of sadness, anger or fear. The sensation may be blurry or incomplete, and yet sometimes even causes a psychosomatic reaction. Memories of an extreme experience, for example, can make the hands sweat or the heart palpitate as though it were happening to you right now.

Your map of thoughts

Experiences, or our memory of them, also give us an inexact reading of the world. Although there is a logical frame to these memories, the logic is that of a Wonderland – a hermetically sealed universe where reality makes sense only within its own boundaries. Any experience leaves some trace or residue that creates a private world and provides reference points for our interpretation of events. These memories form our map of the world: the way it works and the qualities of the people in it. We usually never openly express these shadowy feelings about the world. Although our map is real to us, the memories on which it is based are not true for several reasons. A memory is never an accurate representation of an event, but rather the emotional extraction from it – the sensation or feeling we have been left with. When I think of experiences from my own childhood, my overriding sense is that of warmth, light and sunshine. For you, it may be a different sensation, but it is a sense impression that remains.

The memory is not true because the experience itself was not true to begin with. Every experience has us at its center, viewed from our own perspective. We cannot experience the whole because, as sensory beings, *we are not the whole*. We are already limited by previous experience and by our position at a specific point in space and time. If we were a purely perceiving thing, we would not have a memory of an experience at all; but we are not simple enough to just see, hear or touch. Instead, we interpret through the filter of faulty and incomplete memory.

When I interact with you, I cannot fully understand your perspective any more than I can see the complex interplay of events that led up to our experience. I cannot see the web of life, the endless round of cause and effect that led to the moment when something happened in which I played a part. As you endeavor to pinpoint the moment when one cause has an effect, you will soon discover that you are on an infinite regress, as an endless chain of previous events made possible the moment you are trying to comprehend. Something always precedes your current experience that has an influence on the present.

These half-formed, shadowy memories are not expressed as thoughts; they are feelings, an undefined sense of *something*. These feelings create your map – a filter through which you see the world and color your experience. This filter is the summation of experience, determining the way you react in the present, and how you see the world. It plays out every time you face a situation in the present moment that is reminiscent of a past event.

The filter permeates almost every part of you. You may have a sense that life is hard, people are ungrateful or your spouse doesn't understand you. These thoughts and almost every abstract thought like them have their foundations on nothing more substantial than feelings, which are the afterglow of a memory from a partially understood experience. These feelings may not be apparent, but they color your world, which in turn becomes a reflection of your own thoughts, beliefs and attitudes.

A wonderful Zen story makes the point. A traveler was making his way to the next town when he saw an old man sitting by the side of the road. "What are the people like in the next town?" he asked the old man.

"How were the people in the town you've just left?" the old man responded.

"Oh, they were cold, indifferent and antisocial. That's why I left."

"I'm afraid you'll find the people in the next town are just the same," said the old man.

A few hours later, another traveler walked by, and asked the old man the same question.

"How are the people in the next town?" he asked.

Again, the old man responded, "How were they in the town you've left?" The traveler told him the people in the town were warm, friendly and helpful.

"They're just the same in the next town," said the old man.

Feelings and mega-feelings

Your thoughts and feelings become apparent when somebody says something that sets you off. It could be a word, a phrase, an action or a situation, but whatever the trigger, you suddenly explode. This sudden eruption is often out of all proportion to the circumstance.

You also walk around with a range of concepts that I call mega-feelings, which are the accumulation of a range of partial experiences. These mega-feelings tell you that there is a substantial you and that there is a world "out there." However, as we saw in the previous chapter, this "you" and a world "out there" is not as clearly delineated as you assume. You do not really know who you are any more than you know where you end and a world out there begins.

We will explore these ideas in the second part of the book, when we will look more closely at the past that seems to inhabit us. For now, it is enough to know that you are in its thrall, even though you may not be conscious of the constant past-to-present movement that defines and delineates your reality. As you grow older and accumulate more experience, the filter itself strengthens. Eventually, the accumulated past forms your reality and takes on more meaning and significance than that which is in front of you right now. You do not realize that you are slowly becoming the past, yet many of your thoughts, responses and emotions have their basis in the past – your past.

The Three Types of Experience
Experiences can be broadly categorized as having been good, bad or neutral. Neutral experiences – ones that do not leave an energetic print – are the most common. "Bad" experiences from the past, which leave a trace of sadness, anger or fear, are often reinforced when something similar occurs in the present moment. There is a recognition, as if you see how a situation will play itself out, and the feelings – from incomplete and faulty memory – start to rise up.

Good experiences produce a sudden feeling of joy or unity – an oceanic feeling, as some psychologists describe it – when you feel complete and whole. These latter experiences are invariably the seed of addictive behavior, as we seek to relive that sensation – a process that we shall explore more fully in the second part of this book.

When we are very young, we delight in the moment, as the world unfolds to us. The slightest thing – a worm wriggling in the soil, a dandelion, a bird pecking for food – captivates us. If we have children or grandchildren and they are young enough, you can see this for yourself.

However, this golden age is soon over, and life with its conflicts and troubles quickly rushes in. Researchers at the Kaiser Permanente Hospital in San Diego, California, researching how childhood hurts affect us as adults, have come up with surprising conclusions. The more abuse we suffered as a child – and, by abuse, the researchers include any sort of emotional and physical abuse – the shorter our lives. The way our parents treated us when we were children determines how long we will live.

The research team drew up a list of eighteen possible abuses, which they called "adverse childhood experiences" (ACEs):

1. The parent swore at or insulted the child
2. The parent acted in a way that made the child fear he or she might be physically harmed
3. A parent often slapped, pushed or grabbed the child
4. A parent often hit a child so hard that there were marks or injuries
5. A parent touched or fondled the child
6. A parent wanted the child to touch them in a sexual way
7. A parent attempted some form of sexual intercourse with the child
8. A parent succeeded in having sexual intercourse with the child
9. A parent had a drink or substance abuse problem
10. A parent used street drugs
11. A parent was depressed or mentally ill
12. A parent attempted suicide
13. The mother was sometimes pushed or grabbed
14. The mother was kicked, bitten or hit with a fist
15. The mother was repeatedly hit

16. The mother was threatened with a knife or gun
17. A parent went to prison
18. Parents were separated or divorced

Of their sampling, approximately 12,000 of the 17,000 participants recorded at least one ACE from their childhood. Probably most of us would do the same. How many times did your parents insult you in some way when you were a child? How many times did they belittle you, or tell you that you were not good enough? As you will see, we carry those hurts with us for all our days and eventually they could even kill us. As the researchers discovered, *those participants who suffered six or more ACEs as children died twenty years before a participant who had not recorded any ACEs*. David Brown, the project leader, commented: "It is important to understand that consequences to childhood trauma can extend over an individual's life" (American Journal of Preventive Medicine, 2009; 37: 389-96).

Another study, published around the same time, reached a similar conclusion. Researchers at King's College London tracked the lives of 1,037 participants from their birth in 1972 and 1973 into adulthood. During the first ten years, the researchers noted any adverse experiences the participants might have endured, such as poverty, maltreatment or social isolation. Those participants who suffered three such adverse events as children were more likely to be currently suffering from depression or inflammatory problems – often a precursor to heart disease, arthritis and the like – or already displayed other risk factors, such as high blood pressure, obesity or abnormal cholesterol levels. In fact, the research team reckons that 31 per cent of all cases of depression and 32 per cent of instances of high blood pressure or cholesterol levels are the direct result of an unhappy childhood (Archives of Pediatrics & Adolescent Medicine, 2009; 163: 1135-43).

Childhood abuse of any sort brings on a host of physical diseases. Another study, this time of Jews living in Europe during the Second World War, found that those who were simply aware of the Holocaust – even if they didn't have direct experience of it – were far more likely to develop cancer than were Jews born after the war (Journal of the National Cancer Institute, 2010; 102: 991-2).

In a separate study, researchers have discovered that people who experienced physical abuse as children run a far greater risk of developing osteoarthritis than those who had a happy childhood. The lead researcher Esmé Fuller-Thomson from the University of Toronto said, "This study provides further support for the need to investigate the possible role that childhood abuse plays in the development of chronic disease" (Arthritis Care & Research, 2009; 61: 1554-62).

The past lives in us and through us. Even if it does not cause us physical harm, the past shapes our life. It gives us our picture of the world and the way it works. We live the life we reflect, and that reflection is from the past.

The past and the mirror

We either constantly relive our past or live a "mirror pattern" of it, as I call it, in which we are driven to its opposite. A mother who forces her daughter to take ballet lessons because her own mother refused to allow her lessons when she was young is one typical example.

The woman who grieved

When her youngest child was about to head off to boarding school and a new life away from home, Helen Kirwan-Taylor recalls that she was "on my knees with grief." She was sobbing every night in the bathroom, and she was even thinking of leaving her husband, who'd insisted on boarding school for their child, and returning home to America.

Her sorrow was not for her departing son, however – as she discovered when she participated in a confrontational therapy technique known as the Hoffman Process. It was for her sister, who had been brutally murdered thirty years earlier.

For all those years, Helen had never come to terms with the terrible death of her sister. She had been traumatized by the experience, yet there was no parallel experience in her ordered and happy life. The event could not play itself out in Helen's life.

Finally, an opportunity arose with the sudden loss of her son. This was the closest experience to the death of her sister that Helen could find in her life to undergo a process I call the displaced concept. The feelings are the same, and yet everything else about the experience is changed, other than the central idea of loss.

A famous example of how the past haunts us and creates a mirror pattern comes from the life of the celebrated Victorian writer Charles Dickens. Dickens was fifty-eight when he died at his home at Gad's Hill Place, in Higham, Kent, five days after suffering a stroke in 1870. He was one of the most celebrated authors of his age and has now taken his place in literature as one of the pre-eminent masters of fiction. Although memorable comic characters and grotesques stride through all of his novels, Dickens's own childhood experiences feature most strongly. Most of his books have as a central character a child who is misunderstood, mistreated or in some way mishandled; often the child, who is born into poverty or becomes impoverished, turns out to be, at the very least, a saint or a martyr who dies in tragic circumstances. In the use of children in his fiction, Dickens was often accused of being maudlin and sentimental. However, six years after his death, Dickens's official biographer John Forster revealed that Dickens had taken many of the incidents of childhood deprivation described in the books from his own life.

Dickens said his earliest years were idyllic, although he described himself as "a very small and not-over-particularly-taken-care-of boy." His memory of those times in Portsmouth where he was born remained vivid; he claimed to have a photographic recall of the people and places of that time. The idyll was destroyed when Dickens was just twelve. His father was arrested and imprisoned at the Marshalsea debtor's prison after failing to pay his creditors. Charles went to live in Camden, North London, with a family friend and started work at a blacking factory. He worked ten hours a day under conditions that would appall most of us today, long before the advent of child labor laws, trade unionism and workplace reform. This experience would have a traumatic effect on him. Besides detailing the abuse of children strongly in his fiction, Dickens also spent the hours he was not writing working for the reform of living and labor conditions of the poor.

Many of his friends were astonished at Dickens's prestigious energy; he would write all day, and then spend the night visiting the dives and dens around the London docks. He also produced plays and one-man shows, assuming the roles of some of the best-loved characters from his novels.

For all his life, Dickens feared the debtor's prison that was his father's home for several years. Within a short time of starting to write professionally, he had earned enough money never to need to write another word, but his work rate remained phenomenal. He railed at requests for money from impoverished members of his own family, and even towards the end of his life, when his accumulated wealth was the equivalent of many tens of millions of dollars in today's terms, he still kept an eye open for other job opportunities or supplementary ways of earning an income.

Those close to Dickens believed that his work rate was a major factor in his premature death. He stuck to a grueling tour of his one-man shows, and he collapsed and suffered a mild stroke after one of them nearly a year before he died. However, Dickens did not heed the warning signals, and carried on with his extraordinary work schedule. On the day he suffered the stroke that would prove fatal five days later, Dickens had put in a full day's work on his final uncompleted novel *The Mystery of Edwin Drood*.

Few of us have the genius or energy of Dickens, but most of us can empathize with the demons that haunted him, driving him on to an early death. Whether the patterns from the past are subtle or obvious, they will form your reality. As we saw with Kant and with the quantum physicists, we play an essential role in the creation of the world, but so powerful is our focus that we create our personal world, too. So when you see through the eyes of the past, as if you were looking through a filter, you are bringing the past back to life in the present. Your life *does* become tough, money *does* become hard to come by, keeping a job *is* always difficult – if that was how it used to be and you're unconscious of the movement from the past. Equally, if you have had an abusive husband in the past, you are more than likely to have one again until you wake up to the process and the patterns being created from your past. You have only two options: you remain unconscious or you wake up.

Dickens was driven by the feelings that life is hard and that money is always in short supply. He was haunted by the specter of debt and the debtor's prison, even after he had accumulated a vast fortune. He may not have spent endless hours having such thoughts, but this was the filter through which he saw the world.

The past can be made up of experiences covering long durations of time, such as when Dickens's father was imprisoned for several years, but it is also formed from transitory sensations when something hurtful was said only once or as a result of traumatic or "difficult" experiences that happened infrequently. Irrespective of the duration of the event, the past seems to flatten down into a one-dimensional memory, like an energetic print permanently on repeat. Several of the ACEs listed by the Kasier Permanente researchers did not mention duration; it was sufficient that a parent shouted at you just once or twice for it to be viewed by the researchers as an "adverse event." For a sensitive child, that event could go deep and live on for his entire life. Although the coroner's report stated that Dickens died from a stroke, in fact he died from a past that continued to live on – that became his never-changing present.

Summary: The past infests us. It shapes our reality every day. It becomes our reality. Although it is a very potent force, we are invariably unconscious of its movements and the way it affects us from moment to moment. It creates psychological time, as it shifts the past to a projected future.

Chapter **3**
You out of time

*There is no birth, there is no death; there is no coming, there is
no going; there is no same; there is no different; there is no
permanent self, there is no annihilation. We only think there is.*
Thich Nhat Hanh

You are a creator. You create the dimensions of time and space,
and you create your reality by allowing the past to live through
you. There is also an aspect of you that is outside both time and
space, and you bring this into the world, too. We have all had that
sudden feeling about a place or a person when something
doesn't quite feel right or when we feel immediate warmth, as if
we are "at home." Physicists are beginning to recognize the
intuitive sense of already knowing an experience that is still
unfolding as something that originates outside of space and time.
How could familiarity with a completely new experience be
otherwise?

We don't always have this strange sense of precognition when
we are awake, although we may feel that something isn't quite
right. Most often, a foreboding or presentiment of a future event
happens when we are asleep. On the rare occasions when we
recall our dreams, we sometimes recognize that the images in
them foretell the future. My own experience of this phenomenon
happened just before the start of the Football World Cup of 2010.
I enjoy soccer, but my life is not changed by who wins or loses. I
certainly don't lose sleep over it – although, three days before the
tournament began, I did. I awoke with a start – around five in the
morning, after vividly seeing that England would concede a
simple goal through a stupid goalkeeping error. I clearly saw the

goalkeeper go down for the ball, which rolled under his body, and in his efforts to retrieve it he pushed it further across the line and into the goal. I also "saw" that the score was one-zero to England's opponents, the United States and that the goal happened in the second half.

The following day, I told five people about my dream, adding that if it turned out to be correct, they would know that dreams could foretell the future. On the following Saturday, I settled down to watch the match, and, within five minutes, England had scored. So much for dreams foretelling the future, I thought. Then, in the fortieth minute, one of the US's players hit a long-range, speculative shot at goal. The England goalkeeper got himself behind the ball and then fumbled it, before it went under his body and he pushed it over the line. It happened just as I saw it in the dream! I was wrong about the score and the time of the goal — but the match-defining event happened as if it had been a film on repeat.

My dream of a future event is not unique. In 1927, Irish aeronautical engineer and researcher John (J. W.) Dunne wrote the classic work *An Experiment with Time* (Faber & Faber, London), the result of a study in which he recorded the number of premonitions experienced by a group of participants while they slept. Dunne had trained his recruits to recall their dreams by following back the thought they had the moment they awoke and immediately writing it down. As they practiced, they got better and better at remembering their dreams. During his research, Dunne discovered that dreams could foretell future events, often in vivid and precise detail, just as I had experienced.

Dunne's underlying ambition with his study was to demonstrate that the concept of serial time – one moment following another – is a poor approximation of the truth. For

Dunne, all of time is one vast canvas of now. Our human limitations prevent us from seeing the totality. It could be likened to a book; although the book is there in its entirety, we can take in only one page at a time, and usually sequentially by first reading page 20 before turning to page 21. Nonetheless, page 1 and page 427 are also there at the same time, even though our focus may not be on either of them. Dunne believed that when we sleep, our perception alters, and, in a sense, we can see ahead to page 427.

Many of us have had similar experiences when there is a sudden upset in the expected sequence of serial time and events do not follow their natural course as predicted by the laws of cause and effect. We might be thinking of someone moments before they telephone, sense that someone is looking at us although our head is turned, or have a premonition.

These examples could be dismissed as coincidence, wishful thinking or even the result of an overactive imagination were it not for the vast body of research clearly demonstrating instances when we are out of time and space. Here are some documented examples:

Moments of genius: These sudden flashes of inspiration can be so radical that they push the whole world in a completely new direction. Although they usually happen following a period of intense work and thought, these revolutionary insights are rarely the obvious conclusion of the thought processes that preceded them, or of sustained logical deduction. Instead, radical shifts in scientific thought are often the result of a flash of genius, and the progress of science is as much due to the sudden eureka moment as it is to methodical work.

Albert Einstein was a patent clerk, with the hope of promotion to Technical Expert, Second Class, when he had his flash of genius. He was traveling home in a crowded streetcar that was making its way through the busy streets of Bern one evening in 1904. As it passed the city's famous medieval clock tower, the Zytglogge, the young Einstein suddenly had the realization that time is not an absolute, as Newton said it was, but was relative to the position of the observer and to the speed at which he was traveling. A year later, Einstein published a short paper that mathematically demonstrated this radical idea – which he called the Theory of Special Relativity – along with two other remarkable papers, one of which was to win him the Nobel Prize. His paradigm-shifting insights ushered in the strange world of quantum physics, which would extend Einstein's insight and establish the observer as the determining factor in fixing reality.

Einstein was certainly not alone in having such paradigm-shifting insights. In 1843, Sir William Rowan Hamilton, a professor of mathematics and astronomy at the University of Dublin, was walking across the city's Grougham Bridge when he suddenly "saw" in its entirety his Quaternion Theory, which would transform modern mechanics. In that same moment he also realized it would take a further fifteen years to work out the details of this instantaneous vision.

Nikola Tesla, one of the great geniuses of science, suddenly came up with the idea for alternating current while he was out walking and quoting a passage from Goethe's *Faust*. Otto Loewi claimed to have dreamed how nerve impulses were transmitted chemically, and not electronically, as was then the prevailing view. Loewi said he dreamed the solution, awoke in the middle of the night, hurriedly scribbled down his discovery, and then went back to sleep. The next morning he went to read his notes, and could not make head or tail of the illegible scribbles. That night he had the same dream, and this time when he awoke he wrote more carefully.

Artists are renowned for moments of genius, when they somehow download wonderfully inspiring sounds, words, and images from a place beyond time and space. Beethoven often mentioned in his notebooks that he was transcribing from nature, and that if he did not write down the notes he was hearing, he was sure that someone else eventually would. The Ninth Symphony was not his creation, he claimed, but was already a completed work in the ether, waiting to be transcribed.

Near-death experiences: A US Gallup poll has estimated that up to 12 million Americans have had some experience of life after death, but are too embarrassed to admit to it.

One interesting instance concerned the philosopher A. J. "Freddie" Ayer, whose own rigorous logic would have dismissed claims of an afterlife – until it happened to him. In 1988, when he was 78 years old, Ayer's mental capacities were as sharp as ever, and he was still very much in the business of taking no intellectual prisoners with his no-nonsense rationalism. However, his body was weakening, and he suffered a severe bout of pneumonia while in the United States. He spent ten days in a hospital in New York before flying home to England where he immediately resumed his hectic social life. "Retribution struck me on Sunday, May 30," he related in an article for the *National Review* (October 14, 1988). "I had gone out to lunch, had a great deal to eat and drink, and chattered incessantly. That evening I had a relapse. I could eat almost none of the food which a friend had brought to cook in my house."

Worse was to follow. The next day, he had a long-standing engagement for lunch with a friend, and after making his way home, he went straight to bed without eating. The following day, when Ayer's health had worsened even further, he was taken to University College Hospital in London, put into the intensive care unit, and tended by a young doctor who had been an undergraduate at New College, Oxford, when Ayer had been a lecturer there. "He was so much in awe of me that he forbade me to be disturbed at night, even when the experienced sister and nurse believed it to be necessary," recounted Ayer in his typical immodest way.

Ayer started to recover, but always declined the hospital's food. Used to the better things of life, Ayer was brought fine foods by friends and admirers. One evening, he "carelessly tossed" a slice of smoked salmon into his mouth. It went down the wrong way, and almost immediately, Ayer's heart slowed before stopping completely. Ayer was dead for four minutes while the emergency staff worked frantically to save the life of their most famous patient.

They were successful, and Ayer jolted back to life. The very first words he uttered were, "You are all mad." He said he did not know why he said such a thing, but a few hours later, he told a visitor that while he was dead he saw a bright red light. "I was aware that this light was responsible for the government of the universe," he wrote.

In his *National Review* article, Ayer said that his experiences were "rather strong evidence that death does not put an end to consciousness" and "slightly weakened my conviction that my genuine death will be the end of me, though I continue to hope that it will be." The experience certainly seemed to have mellowed the usually acerbic Ayer; as his wife noted, "Freddie has been so much nicer since he died."

Ayer did indeed die thirteen months later, in June 1989, but there remained one final mystery. It seems that Ayer did not apply his usual rigorous standards to the account of his near-death experience (NDE) given to friends and the readers of the *National Review*. Years later the young doctor, Dr Jeremy George, who attended Ayer – the one apparently in awe of the great philosopher – revealed that Ayer had disclosed that he had seen the "supreme being" during his four minutes in the death state. "I'm afraid I'm going to have to revise all my books and opinions," he apparently added. This was something that Ayer had never recounted to anyone else. To do so would have thrown into question his life-long philosophical stance.

Neuroscientists dismiss near-death experiences as the result of overactivity in a brain starved of oxygen. However, many cases of NDEs happen to patients who are completely devoid of any physical and mental activity and so are clinically dead. The starved-brain theory also cannot explain the many cases of "dead" patients who continue to observe exactly what is happening in the emergency room and can relate the sequence of events in precise detail after they have been revived. In one case, a patient who "saw" the nurse remove his dentures when he was clinically dead was able to remind her where she had put them after he had been jolted back to life.

Life-support patients: Patients who are clinically dead and need life-support in order to keep their organs functioning often retain a degree of consciousness. A study by Cambridge University discovered that a patient on life-support continues learning. In a simple experiment, the researchers played a tone immediately before blowing air into the patient's eye. After doing this several times, the research team noticed that the patient would start to blink in anticipation of the puff of air when he heard the tone.

This experiment demonstrates that even a patient in a vegetative state has a memory and learns to anticipate events (Nature Neuroscience, 2009; 12: 1222-3).

Spontaneous remission: Most diseases develop through a series of recognized stages. Cancer, for example, has four phases, and orthodox medicine maintains that it will invariably result in death unless the patient is successfully treated. However, cancer specialists accept that some cases will spontaneously regress, which means the tumors mysteriously disappear. Nobody knows how common spontaneous remission is, although Professor Uwe Hobohm of the University of Applied Sciences in Giessen, Germany, reckons it may occur in one out of every 10,000 cases of cancer. Researchers in Ontario, Canada, suggest that Hobohm has underestimated the rate. In their study, 145 cancer patients out of approximately 10,000 reviewed had had no medical treatment whatsoever. Of those, 35 per cent were alive five years later, and the average survival rate was forty-seven months. In addition, 70 per cent of those whose cancer did not spread were living five years later. The overall survival rate among women was 45 per cent and, among men, 36 per cent (The Canadian Medical Association Journal, 1965; 92: 647-51).

Whatever the true rate of spontaneous remission, the numbers are inevitably low in any study because the phenomenon is so hard to prove. Virtually all cases of cancer are treated by chemotherapy, radiotherapy or surgery – and an instance of spontaneous remission is considered valid only if there has been no medical intervention whatsoever. Instances of spontaneous remission tend to be noticed only in those rare cases when the patient does not report the cancer until it is too advanced for medical intervention, and the patient, sent home to die, instead recovers. The event is also grossly underreported because the patient usually doesn't get back in touch with the oncologist. If he does, the doctor does not record the recovery, usually because he does not believe it.

Remote viewing: Remote viewing is the ability to "see" places or things that are miles away or hidden from view. The remote viewer is usually given just a map or grid reference, and he uses it in order to zero in on the location in order to "see" it. The CIA experimented with remote viewing during the Cold War, and researchers at the Princeton Engineering Anomalies Research (PEAR) laboratory have systematically studied it through 336 formal trials, invariably using a method they called "precognitive remote perception". The remote viewer, seated in the PEAR laboratory, would be asked not only to name the destination of a fellow participant, but also to do so hours – and sometimes days – before his partner arrived, and often before the partner himself knew where he was going.

In one case of precognitive viewing, the viewer described and drew a train station that the other participant would visit thirty-five minutes later. In another example, the viewer had the "strange but persistent" image of the other participant standing in a large bowl. Forty-five minutes later, the participant arrived at the massive curved dome-like structure of the radio telescope in Kitt Peak, Arizona. Other scientists have demonstrated in a variety of studies that people have the ability to see into the future. The late parapsychologist Charles Honorton of the Maimonides Medical Center in Brooklyn, New York, carried out a meta-analysis of studies of "future viewing", which usually involved predicting the symbols on a card or the numbers that would be thrown with dice. The combined result of 309 trials, involving approximately two million separate tests, was so robustly positive that the likelihood that they could have occurred by chance were ten million billion billion to one (Radin, D. *The Conscious Universe*, New York: HarperEdge, 1997).

Telepathy: The psychologist Stanley Krippner, professor of psychology at Saybrook Graduate School, San Francisco, and the psychiatrist Montague Ullman, who founded the Dream Laboratory at the Maimonides Medical Center, carried out a series of experiments demonstrating that thoughts could be transmitted by one volunteer to a sleeping participant, who would incorporate the ideas or images of the transmitted thought into his dreams. Researchers at the University of California independently corroborated the results, recording an 84 per cent accuracy rate. The odds for that level of success occurring by chance alone were 250,000 to one.

The man who should have died

The journalist Robert Blair Kaiser, a war reporter in Vietnam, and a former correspondent with Time *magazine and* Newsweek, *was behind the wheel of his car, pulling out of his driveway. Suddenly, as he said later, "I was awakened from my dreamy preoccupation by the sight of a speeding car bearing down on me, not five feet away on my left. I knew I was a dead man. All of a sudden, that car was on my right. . . there was no way he could have missed crashing into me, no way he could have steered aside. His car had flashed through my car, his steel and glass and rubber passing through my steel and glass and rubber like a ray of light through a pane of alabaster"* (Daily Nation, *March 2001). According to natural laws, the two cars should have collided as one car*

> *was traveling at speed and was just five feet away when Kaiser saw it approaching. Yet it did not happen.*

Premonitions: The researchers Cassandra Eason, Sylvia Browne and others have investigated the bond that seems to exist between mothers and children, which does not appear to be dependent on time and space. Eason recalls one story of a young mother who left her small child for the first time with a minder to go to the cinema with her husband. After a short while, she told her husband that she could smell smoke and that their baby was in danger. The husband tried to placate her, believing her fears were just those of an over-anxious mother. However, the woman was insistent, so the couple abandoned the cinema and rushed home – to discover a fire that had started in the downstairs room, the babysitter asleep, and the baby's room full of smoke (*The Psychic Power of Children*, W Foulsham & Co, Slough, 2005).

The holistic doctor and author Larry Dossey tells a similar story concerning a woman called Amanda in his book *The Power of Premonitions* (Dutton, New York, 2009). Amanda had dreamed that the chandelier in the next room had fallen from the ceiling onto her sleeping infant's crib and crushed the baby. In the dream, she observed that a clock in the baby's room read 4:35 am and the wind and rain were hammering against the windows at the time the chandelier had crashed.

Extremely upset, Amanda woke up her husband and told him her dream. He insisted that it was meaningless and urged her to go back to sleep. However, the dream was so vivid and frightening that Amanda went into the baby's bedroom room and brought the sleeping baby into their bed. Soon she was woken up by a loud crash in the baby's room. She rushed in to see that the chandelier had fallen and crushed the crib – that the clock in the room read 4:35, and that wind and rain were howling outside. Her dream premonition was camera-like in detail, taking in the specific event, the precise time, and even a change in the weather.

Dean Radin, senior scientist at the Institute of Noetic Sciences in Petaluma, California, who has tested thousands of cases of what he calls "presentiments", believes that the experience is relatively common. He began researching the phenomenon in the 1980s after a friend told him a remarkable story. The friend would always leave the sixth chamber of his gun empty while he was cleaning it, but on one occasion, he had the overwhelming feeling that he should not put the bullet back in the chamber afterwards. Several weeks later, he was in a drunken argument with his father-in-law who suddenly reached for the gun. If the bullet had been in the chamber, Radin's friend would have died that day (*The Power of Premonition*, ibid).

Out of Body Experiences (OBEs): The late sociologist and author Ian Currie, former professor of York University in Toronto, discovered that approximately 20 per cent of people have experienced the phenomenon of looking down at their own body from an aerial perspective. In one case of a woman who claimed to have frequent out-of-body experiences, researchers placed a number on a small piece of paper in a script so small that a person could read it only if they were inches away. The piece of paper was stuck to the ceiling, some twelve feet from the bed where she lay. She was monitored throughout the night while she slept, and, although she never left the bed, in the morning she was always able to tell the researchers the number they had put on the ceiling (*You Cannot Die*, Somerville House, 1978).

Reincarnation: The late Ian Stevenson, a former professor of psychiatry at the University of Virginia, put his academic standing at risk by carrying out exhaustive research into reincarnation, investigating thousands of cases over forty years. In every instance, he explored alternative possibilities before deciding if the case could be explained only by reincarnation.

In one case, a boy in Beirut recalled being a 25-year-old mechanic who had been knocked down and killed some years previously. The boy knew the names of his sisters, parents and cousins in this earlier life – and even the name of the driver who knocked him down. The details identically matched an accident that had happened years before the boy was born to a family unknown to him. Stevenson explored the case further and was satisfied that he was not the victim of fraud and that the boy was not lying or mistaken. Eventually the case joined the three thousand others that Stevenson had conservatively categorized as "cases suggestive of reincarnation" and "cases of the reincarnation type.

I call these phenomena ESTs – Events outside of Space and Time. From all of this evidence it seems indisputable that people have the potential to have experiences outside of serial time and their immediate space. Sometimes the law of cause and effect is violated, and events happen out of sequence. When they do, we call them miracles.

Despite the voluminous amount of research and evidence that supports ESTs, skeptics still doubt that they actually happen and dismiss them as cases of fraud, suggestion, or self-delusion, or as so trivial as to merit discounting. The paranormal researcher Michael Schmicker calls this approach "scientism," which he describes as "a philosophy of materialism, masquerading as scientific truth."

Two women who were healed by a miracle

Events outside Space and Time (ESTs) violate one or more of the natural laws, and they happen every day and to almost everyone some time or another, even to me. My own EST concerned my mother, Edie, who at the time was aged 78. I visited her and my father one Sunday when someone accidentally brushed against her breast while walking past her. She immediately bent double, clearly in enormous pain. She confessed that she had been nursing her breast for nearly two years, wrapping it in bandages, and hoping the open sores would just go away.   The rest of my family and I insisted she see the family doctor the following day, which she reluctantly agreed to do. According to her account, she said she had never seen a doctor react in such a way before. When she had shown him her breast, all he could see was an open red sore, which had enveloped the entire breast, and he recoiled in disgust and horror. This was breast cancer in its final stages, and he confided to my father that she had, at most, three months to live. I was not prepared to accept that prognosis. I had been the publisher of a health journal called What Doctors Don't Tell You, *and I knew there were many proven healing modalities that just might work.*

Within a week, we had booked an appointment with a qualified doctor who, nonetheless, was pioneering alternative cancer therapies. He examined my mother's breast, and he, too, confirmed that this was cancer in its final stages. He immediately put my mother on a drip, which was delivering very high levels of hydrogen peroxide and vitamin C intravenously. He also insisted on a radical change of diet.

My mother dutifully traveled the sixty-three miles to his surgery twice a week for her infusion, and slowly over the months the breast started to heal. Six months later the family doctor bumped into her in the street and genuinely thought he had seen a ghost. He could not believe his eyes, and like most people who cannot believe the evidence in front of them, he insisted on tests. My mother subjected herself to a mammogram that revealed that, indeed, the breast was completely free of cancer.

So did the vitamin C and hydrogen peroxide mix kill the cancer? Clearly so. However, something else also happened. When we first were given the diagnosis and prognosis, everyone in the family expressed their enormous love for Edie; as she was a woman who had selflessly given all her life, these declarations were nothing less than the truth. For the first time, I "love bombed" my mother with messages and flowers. My father, who enjoyed spending money about as much as a banker relishes a zero-bonus year, suddenly raided his savings and willingly paid for all the expensive treatments. This was the highest expression of love my mother had ever witnessed.

The esteemed child-development researcher Joseph Chilton Pierce reported a similar experience. In his landmark book, The Crack in the Cosmic Egg *(Park Street Press, 2002), Pierce revealed how his own wife succumbed to breast cancer, just as almost every female relative had before her. Despite the close attention of oncologists, his wife was given weeks to live, after nearly every vital organ of hers was removed, burned or permanently harmed. Like me, Pierce was also not prepared to accept the prognosis, and he spent night and day whispering positive and healing words to his comatose wife, who had been sent home to die. This was an epic labor of love, and at the end, Pierce must have been utterly exhausted, having denied himself proper sleep or food for three weeks. However, the prize was beyond value. His wife started to make a full recovery, as though she had been reprogrammed by Pierce's confident and positive code to be well.*

He adds: "Paranormal research has used the process of science to prove the existence of a variety of phenomena that simply doesn't fit within scientism's philosophy of materialism. If evidence conflicts with the philosophy, the evidence shouldn't be dismissed; instead, the philosophy should be revised" (Best Evidence, Writer's Club Press, Lincoln 2000).

Psychologist William James put it another way. It takes only one white crow to disprove the notion that all crows are black. Similarly, it takes just one legitimate case of EST from the many thousands collated to demonstrate that we are not always trapped in a determined universe of space and time. In my view, this has been proven beyond any doubt.

Summary: Although you create time and space, you also live outside of both. This is the third, and final, element that makes you "you." It is also the most mysterious, because it throws up intriguing metaphysical questions about what it is that you are, whether you survive death and whether we are purely the body, subject to inevitable aging and illness. Although extreme examples do not happen to everyone, all of us have known moments that seem to occur when the laws of time or space, or those of both, are violated. This self that lives outside of space-time is also the creative impulse, as we have seen in instances of intuitive leaps and genius.

Chapter **Four**
You and time

*Man is an animal suspended in webs of significance
he himself has spun.*

Clifford Geertz

Neuroscience tells us that any sense of an "I" is the result of complex neural firings in the brain. These firings occur between the three areas of the brain: the old, reptilian part, responsible for survival; the midbrain, where emotions are processed; and the new part, or neocortex, where we think, understand language and speech, and appreciate music. According to this view, the sense of self may seem substantial and unchanging, yet it is fragile, a phantom that can be altered through illness, brain injury, and aging. When the body dies, the brain dies with it. As a result, you die, too, as does everything you thought you were.

Underpinning this is the belief that you are simply a body. The sense of an "I" comes from the workings of the brain, which, in turn, is in the body. It would be reasonable to suppose, in that case, that we would do everything in our power to preserve and protect the body. The principal role of the "I" would be as the body's guardian.

This does not always happen, as we see with people who are drug addicts, alcoholics or smokers. Something in them seems to turn against the well-being of the body, and appears intent on either actively destroying it, or on satisfying a need that is greater than its preservation. We are also prepared to sacrifice our body for a greater cause, such as in time of war or for a religious belief. This, too, suggests that we are more than a body.

On a more mundane level, we see contradictions in the way

people behave. We often say one thing, but privately believe another. We contradict ourselves or constantly change our mind. We suffer from stress and anxiety, which suggests there are different aspects of the self, between which there are tensions and competing demands. For example, we can become stressed or anxious if we are doing one thing, but wanting to do another.

Our investigations in the first three chapters also indicate you are more than one thing. Kant showed us that we have a special relationship with the world and that it is we – whoever "we" are – who make the world what it is. Einstein and his discoveries took this further, ushering in the world of quantum physics and the primacy of the observer as the cocreator of his world. With the help of a piece of smoked salmon, we also found that we appear to extend beyond space and time, and even to survive death. Charles Dickens and the thousands who have taken part in important research projects into adverse events in childhood, colored in the rest of the story of you by demonstrating the importance of the past in defining who it is that we think we are, the world we live in and what we perceive as reality.

So here is a quick resume:

"You" cannot be one thing: Most neurologists and biologists agree that we are only one thing: a body. Yet, if this were so, Professor Ayer couldn't have been both dead in his hospital bed and at the same time capable of registering a light any more than other dead patients float above the bed and afterward are able to recount exactly what was said and done while emergency crews were working on their bodies. Similarly, you cannot be just a body and, at the same time, be capable of influencing something thousands of miles away, just with your thoughts. Moreover, if you are only a brain and its appendages, how are you aware of

visitors and their conversations or able to learn simple skills, when your brain is comatose?

You are not always governed by time and space: Although it appears that we exist in a universe where time moves forward serially and space exists as an objective dimension, many instances suggest this is not always the case. Every EST, including premonitions, forebodings, and remote viewing, flouts the laws of time or space, or both.

The laws of cause and effect do not always govern you: A constant and immutable law of science is that every cause has an effect. Nevertheless, the myriad of examples of ESTs that we have already examined suggest that these laws can be violated.

We have a special relationship with the world: Kant was one of the first to realize that the world is relative to us. His early insight has since been supported by innumerable studies in the field of quantum physics. So special is this relationship, in fact, that it is difficult to say where "you" end and the world "outside" begins, as the science of epigenetics is discovering. This special relationship explains why we are able to have intuitive leaps and make extraordinary discoveries about the world that are not apparent to our senses.

We are co-creators of our reality: Quantum physics has demonstrated that we imprint time and space on the unknown, the infinite, and the eternal. We also create our own reality through our past, as happened to Charles Dickens and indeed happens to almost every one of us.

We are as much the past as we are the present: We are governed as much by the past as we are by the present – in many cases, more so. This past makes itself apparent through feelings we have, even though they are rarely perceptible to us. Feelings are also the building blocks of the concepts we have about the world and ourselves.

So, who are you? Every available explanation fails to capture the full richness of who we are, and no one definition explains the range of phenomena that we experience as human beings. All along, I believe the problem has been in looking for just one definition of the self. As long as we do so, we are never going to come up with an answer that satisfies all experiences associated with the self.

Philosophers have never been able to agree on what it is that we are:

● Plato said we are essentially a soul

● Aristotle posited that we are a body without a soul

● John Locke concluded that any sense of self comes from memory

● Descartes claimed that we are a thinking thing that is separate from the body and survives death

● David Hume outlined that the self is merely an agglomeration of sensual inputs

● Spinoza surmised that we are a part of nature

● Schopenhauer explained that we are a blind will to live

● Nietzsche argued that we are a will to power,

and so on throughout the centuries.

Paradoxically, all of them were correct, in part, but ultimately they were wrong – because we are not just one thing. Clearly, we are more than what we are told. There is more going on in us than merely a brain in a body.

PART **TWO**
YOUR THREE SELVES

Chapter **Five**
Your Three Selves

Mass and energy are both but different manifestations of the same thing – a somewhat unfamiliar conception for the average mind.

Albert Einstein

You are the sum of Three Selves, or energy centers. Although each center has its own vibrational pattern, there is overlap between all three, and the boundaries are fluid while the body is alive. As an energy center, each sends out a pulse, and the dominant pulse determines who you are at any one time. You could be fully present in the moment or thinking and worrying about the past – as increasingly happens as you age and become more time-heavy – or have sudden uprush of joy and a feeling of unity with everything.

Neuroscience might suggest that these selves are merely the three parts of the physical brain. It is important to stress that my model is an energetic one, not a physical description. Energy is the ultimate reality of the universe, as Albert Einstein famously demonstrated, and the physical universe is merely energy that we sense. It may be that the three-part brain is the physical apparatus through which the energetic one expresses itself, but this does not concern us. We must move beyond the physical – materialist – description, which has assumed that, by identifying and naming specific parts in the world, it can explain the mystery of you and the richness of the human experience. This approach to understanding is as satisfying and meaningful as attempting to learn about the beauty of music through the diagram of a violin.

Your three energetic selves

The Present time-body: This relates to the body and the world, and to living in time and space. Everything in the world – other people, the flora and fauna, our sun and the stars, the buildings, the cars – is within the Present time-body, as are you as a body and a brain. It is strange to realize that the universe is a self. It is not *your self*, however, but the universal self that is expressing itself in and through each and every body. This process creates a feeling of a personal experience, which includes me – as an undefined entity – my body and, by extension, my possessions. As we saw in the opening chapter, this self creates time and space – and finds itself in it as a player in a drama that it has written, produced and staged (and observed as the audience).

It also completely identifies with its own creation. Indeed, it so much believes in its creation that it sees itself as separate and its body as different to all the other bodies it sees around it. You get a sense of this total immersion if you've ever been to a movie and become so engrossed in it that you forget yourself and enter the drama on the screen. Actually, you're doing that every moment of your life, and you've forgotten that you are both infinite and limited by space, eternal and mortal, endlessly creative and restricted, completely free and a being caught in the web of cause and effect. Where "you" are is determined by the dominant time-body or center that creates your sense of self at any time.

The Present time-body is the center that is most understood by the sciences, including physics, astrophysics, biology, and medicine, and it deals with the world of concepts, of things and stuff, of the measurable and definable. The Present time-body also includes the intangible – our fears, anger, rage, hunger, thirst, and sexual desire in the moment – which continues to reverberate within this center as an emotional footprint. Just as a dog might be fearful of other dogs after a savage attack, so the Present time-body carries a resonance of a previous experience. However, as we saw in the first part, we are more than the present moment; we are as much the past as we are the "now," and it is the past that shapes us and our world, motivates us, makes us go to war, and may even eventually kill us.

The Past time-body: This is the second of your Three Selves, and it stands between "you" and a rich life by preventing a feeling of connection to everyone and everything else. It is the depository of experience – but of a special type. It concerns those experiences that have not been fully witnessed and resolved at the time; as a result, they continue to live on as a vibration in the Past time-body.

The Past time-body itself is made up of three layers, because there are different memory, or energetic, forms. *The Narrative Past* is the story of the self, including your name, where you live, your culture and nationality. *The Knowledge Past* is the problem-solving center, which remembers how to build a shelf or fix a problem on a PC. Finally, *the Psychological Past* is the storehouse of experiences that are not fully witnessed, resolved or understood. Some psychologists call this the unconscious or the subconscious, but far from being unconscious, our Past is constantly seeking to be understood in a fully conscious moment and will create repeated patterns in order to do so.

The Potential center: Why is it that we seem to create the life – and, indeed the world – that we focus on? Reality is a consensus view; you find that which you seek, you create that which you discover. This is possible only because you are also made up of the Potential center,

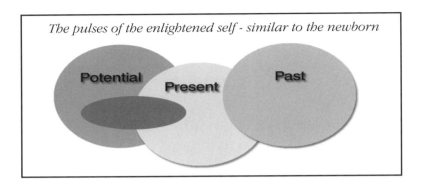

The pulses of the enlightened self - similar to the newborn

the creative force and the potential field of all possibilities. One analogy is to see this center as the canvas, while the other two – the Present and the Past time-bodies – provide the paint and the brushwork. All three combine to make "you", the artist.

The German philosopher Martin Heidegger said the greatest marvel was that there was life at all, when it was much more likely that there should be nothing. The miracle of life is made possible by the Potential center. Through the Present time-body, this unified field expresses itself in space and time as separate and multiple representations of life. While we live exclusively in – and through – the Present and Past time-bodies, we are blind to the unity of life; instead, we see its apparent diversity through the eyes of an individual, who is separate from others. It is a phenomenon I call Universal Subjectivity – we all think we are having a separate experience although none of us actually is.

Figure 1: The chief characteristics of the Three Selves

Present	Constant change and flux
Past	Repetition. A desire for constancy.
Potential	Continual renewal. The field of all possibility.

Figure 2: The chief expressions of the Three Selves

	Highest expressions	**Lowest expressions**
Present	Sympathy; Trust; Logical thought	Violence; Anger
Past	Empathy; Compassion	Hatred; Envy; Morbid Fear
Potential	Love (a sense of unity)	

Figure 3: The Three Selves in time and space

	In space/time	**Survives death**
Present	Yes	No
Past	No	For a period
Potential	No	Yes

At the death of the body, the Present time-body dies with it – and so, to that extent, neuroscience's view about your dying when your body does is correct. But the Past time-body lives on independently of the body for a period, and the length of that period is determined by the extent of the Past time-body's identification with the body. The Potential center neither lives nor dies, as it is beyond both experiences.

Change and permanence

Using the model of the three time bodies, you might be able to see the pivotal point of Buddhism and Taoism. Both philosophies tell us that the constant of life is suffering while we see ourselves as a permanent, fixed self. The world is always changing, and yet we either want things to stay as they are, or we build a wall of material things to protect us from the vicissitudes of life.

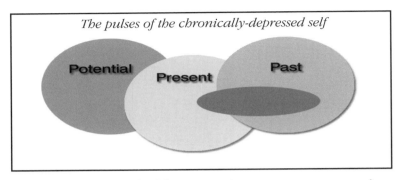

The pulses of the chronically-depressed self

Potential   Present   Past

However, we cannot build certainty. At any moment we can lose our money, our home, our husband or wife.

We also have to understand exactly what is having this experience. If we see ourselves as a constant self, we will suffer precisely because this idea is a fiction. Not only are we part of life that is in flux, but we are that life itself. However, until we become conscious of the time-bodies, our sense of who we are changes, depending on the dominant pulse. You might smell the scent of a flower one moment, then think of someone who upset you the next, then realize the beauty and wonder of the garden in which you find yourself. Each of those contrasting moods comes from one of the time-bodies, and the change can happen in moments.

The concept of a consistent self – the "I" that records, interprets, and reacts – is described as the ego by some, who generally believe that the ego dies with the body, or as the soul by others, who imagine that this constant self survives death. While something survives you, it is not the "you" that you think it is! It is an impersonal self – but, then, there never was anything personal about life, not even "your" life.

Applying the *Time-Light* model to the precepts of Buddhism, we see that the Present time-body's constant is change, while the

Past time-body possesses an urge for repetition and a desire to have more of the same. As we shall see, this urge from the Past time-body is a process in order to seek understanding and completion. Only when that is achieved will the pulses from the Past time-body diminish, and the patterns from the past disappear.

You are the sum of one center that creates time and space and a sense of self based on the body (the Present time-body); another that reinforces the sense of a separate self through the past (the Past time-body); and a third that is the creative field of all possibility, outside of time and space (the Potential center). While the Past time-body dominates, you are more the past than the present moment, and your experiences will tend to be a reiteration and a reliving of experience. You will also have a keener sense of separation, even isolation, from the world and from others. You will not be completely "there" attending in the present and so not be fully seeing and responding to the truth of the now. Typical symptoms of a past-dominant life are aimless thinking or mental chatter, mild depression, anxiety, a sense of worthlessness and a feeling that life is pointless. Its extreme expression is despair.

As your life is on constant repeat through the pulses of the Past time-body, you will manifest patterns in your life – the same sort of thing tends to happen to you over and over – and you may have addictions. An addiction is not only a dependency on alcohol, drugs or gambling, but also repeated behavioral patterns that are possibly less damaging, or noticeable. They show up as a personality "tic", a tendency always to do things the same way, or a common reaction to a person or the world that is similar in different circumstances.

Everything is new in the now; if you lived entirely in the Present time-body you would respond appropriately to each new experience as it arose, and you would feel at one with it all. Even so, someone whose Present time-body is dominant would not necessarily be aware of the Potential center and the unity of all things.

Here are some examples of how the pulses may vary from person to person, or from time to time:

Small child: Mainly Present, some Potential
Adolescent: Mainly Present, some Past, a little Potential
Adult: Some Present, mainly Past, a little Potential
Addict/Depressed person: Mainly Past, little Present, almost no Potential
Saint/realized person: Mainly Potential, some Present, a little Past

Responding and reacting

As we age, we become more the past – the Psychological Past in particular – which creates patterns from previous experiences that were not fully understood or resolved at the time, and that are lived out again in the present. Instead of responding, we react because the experience is familiar, and all the old emotions of fear, anger, or rejection well up again. It's as if we're saying, "I know what's happening here, I know what to expect from this

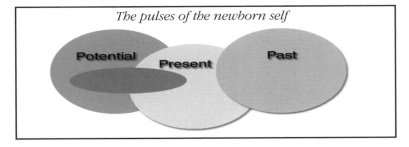

The pulses of the newborn self

Potential   Present   Past

person/situation." In truth, we do not know what is going to happen because, in the present moment, everything is new and in flux. We only think we know because the situation has similarities to a previous experience.

A reaction invariably adds fuel to the flame, and the situation often escalates as a result. Let's take as an example a husband whose behavior is constantly being challenged by his wife. This challenging creates an immediate pulse from the Psychological center of the Past time-body that, almost instantaneously, is interpreted as a feeling or emotion, and then a series of thoughts. The reaction escalates the situation, whereas a response – the appropriate action in the present moment, and commensurate with the situation – would dissipate any energy around the exchange.

Suppose that instead of *reacting* with a "You're always trying to correct me. What about all your problems – let's look at those, shall we?" the husband was conscious enough – that is, conscious to the pulse from the past – to instead *respond* with a, "I see my behavior is upsetting to you, as you're always pointing it out to me. What is it about it that so upsets you and how do you think I could do better?"

Few of us respond. Instead, we react to events in the present moment, which means that we are bringing the past to bear on the here and now. The present, which is rich with possibility, is constantly sabotaged by patterns from the past. As you get older, so the burden grows, and the patterns become denser. Eventually, you either become time-heavy, which quickens the death of the physical body, or you finally wake up to the pulse of feelings from the Past time-body.

If you do wake up, the Past-to-Present movement loses its power. You start to become *Time-Light*, and you live more in the

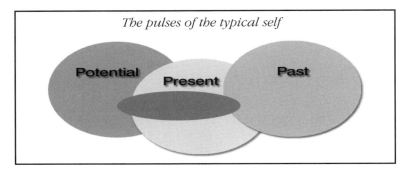

The pulses of the typical self

Potential

Present

Past

present moment. You allow the pulses from the Present time-body to dominate, and you become more at one with the world and with everyone in it. The diminishing of the pulses from the Past time-body also allows the Potential center to "come through," and you, in the present moment, get a sense of unity, eternity and infinity. In that moment, you are natural, truly – and finally – a human being.

When we are children, we start out as *Time-Light*. We have had few experiences that we have not completely understood, and we live to an extent outside of time and space. We are in our own world – but the world "out there" is also our home. Because the Potential center is much more to the fore – its pulse is dominant – children actually are more outside of time and space than are most adolescents and adults. Unless the child is abused – when pulses from the Present and Past centers start to dominate because the child is unable to fully comprehend what is happening to him – life seems to have an eternal glow, which we forever try to retrieve when we get older. Because we never seem to recreate those golden, timeless days of childhood, we compensate with cars, houses, career success and money, not realizing that these make us more time-heavy and take us even further away from the idyll of the Potential center.

The pulses

All three centers communicate via pulses or waves, which are then interpreted into thought forms by the brain, especially by its ability to conceptualize. This gives interpretation and substance to pulses that are derived from a painful or difficult experience, and they become expressions of fear, worry, doubt. The harnessing of the conceptual mind also begins to create patterns in the world that become your reality.

Most pulses derive from neutral experiences, which do not involve a feeling of hurt, fear or sadness, and these come from the Narrative and Knowledge past centers. That is how we make our way in the world and how we solve problems.

However, the process becomes toxic when we create concepts from pulses from the Psychological past; past hurts and disappointments are given flesh by the conceptual mind, which defines them into a sense of a "you" that is substantial, real, and permanent. However, this sense of you separates you from the world, and the acid of past hurts dissolves the delicate thread that unites you to the field of all being. The process of pulse-to-concept-to-substantial-you is a hopeless, reiterative loop, which is on constant repeat in the present in a vain attempt to be finally understood. It is hopeless because the past can never be recreated in the Present; continuity and flux just don't mix. When pulses from the Narrative and Psychological time-bodies fuse, we can have war, terror, and conflict, as national, racial or religious identity mix with a sense of past hurt and grievance.

Together, these three layers of the Past time-body go towards the creation of our sense of self. Without the Past center, the Present would be pure consciousness – an observation of just what is in front of you at this moment. Is your father shouting at you right now? Of course not, all that is happening is the kettle boiling, or a bird singing in your garden, or music playing on the radio. Yet our father is still shouting at us through the psychological layer of our Past time-body.

Conversely, if we allow the pulses of the Potential center to dominate, we have a rich sense of oneness and unity with everything around us. We are vessels that bring unity – or love – into a world that appears to be separate with multiple forms.

All of us walk around with a certain identity – I am Jewish, or Christian, English or American – and these are memory forms from another part of the Past time-body, the Narrative center. These truths and memory forms are usually harmless enough and become a possible threat to others and ourselves only if they are mixed with the hurts of the Psychological past.

The Knowledge past is the most important of the three in terms of navigating your way around the world. You could not live a properly functioning life without it, as you would not know anything about the world. You wouldn't know your name, where you lived, how to drive a car or what you had learned.

The brain, the subconscious and the selves
Most neuroscientists hold to the theory that different areas of the brain are responsible for specific functions, such as memory or motor skills. However, many are beginning to understand the brain's complexity, and that a more accurate model for its workings is a hologram, where every part contains the whole. New brain research supports this view. Instead of seeing the brain as a hierarchy of sections, neuroscientists are beginning to realize that the brain's areas "talk" to each other by way of circular loops in a distributed network, similar to the way that the internet is constructed. The discovery, made by researchers from the National

Institutes of Health, suggests the brain does not have higher or lower centers of conscious thought, but works as a decentralized network. As a result, an area of the brain often compensates for another that may have been damaged (Proceedings of the National Academy of Sciences, 2010; doi: 10.1073/pnas.1009112107).

Even this explanation may not go far enough. If matter is viewed ultimately as energy that is palpable to the senses, then the brain becomes merely the receiving organ and interpreter of energy – and is itself a different expression of energy.

Some psychologists and therapists argue that phobias and trauma emanate from our subconscious or unconscious mind. However, I contend that they don't, because *you do not have an unconscious or subconscious mind*. It is a myth that we have come to accept through repeated telling, one to which some schools of psychology still cling. Instead of a buried area of the mind that we don't have conscious access to, we have the Past center and its three layers. Within them, experiences reside as an energetic store. We may be unconscious of the movements from the Past center, but that does not mean they reside in an actual "unconscious". On the contrary, everything seeks to become conscious, to reach an understanding, to have an end in that knowing.

The drive to greater understanding is the one common theme of humanity throughout the ages. It is not only demonstrated in the sciences, but also in the arts, when the artist either seeks his or her own understanding or wants us to understand his or her vision. Your past is no different; it is part of the energy flow towards understanding – yet it can reach its completion, as a fully understood experience, only in time and space, in the here and now. This moment is always the proving ground, the crucible in which an experience is either resolved or allowed to continue creating its patterns.

The woman who loved cupcakes

Joanna loved cupcakes. Indeed, she loved all the foods that were bad for her – and it showed. She was always fighting the flab, and rarely went down a dress size – except when she summoned up enormous willpower and went on a diet. She'd tried all the diets and the latest fads. They worked for a while, but she was always going back to the cupcakes, and so the pounds would go right back on again.

But what kept drawing her back to the "bad foods," especially when she knew – in her rational brain, at least – that she would put on more weight, and she'd hate herself for it?

She decided to find out, and she visited a local hypnotist who was known for her abilities to help people with weight issues. Joanna doubted that she would be able to "go under", but she did – although the experience was not as she expected. She was conscious, and she "knew" she was being hypnotized, and yet she could not help herself. When the hypnotist told her that her eyelids were getting heavy, they started to fall. When the hypnotist told her to raise her right arm, she did, even though she tried to fight it.

After a few simple exercises, the hypnotist invited Joanna to go back to her earliest memories, especially any that were associated with food. Almost immediately, Joanna saw herself as a five-year-old, sitting in the kitchen of her grandparents. The grandparents were arguing; the grandmother was accusing her husband of having a girlfriend. Joanna was waiting to have a meal with them, but the grandmother was letting the food burn on the stove. From there, other memories of food and emotional issues – ones that she had "forgotten" – started to arise.

Hypnotism is a good technique for accessing the oldest memories from the Psychological past, allowing them to rise up without any interpretation or justification from the conceptual mind. It allows you to see the memory clearly, the pulse of the trapped emotion, the experience you can't understand. In Joanna's case, she was just a five-year-old in the center of an emotional crisis in the family.

Finally, at the age of 43, Joanna was able to see the whole situation – the little girl that she then was, the emotional turmoil of her grandparents – and forgive them and herself. As soon as she did, the desire for cupcakes vanished in the forgiveness that crossed time and space.

All desires are equal

Some of us who realize that money in the bank will not scratch the metaphysical itch of feeling hollow and unfulfilled instead turn to religion and spirituality. However, until we wake up to the Past-to-Present movement, we are in danger of merely adding to the weight of the past. *There is no qualitative difference between wanting to be a millionaire and wanting spiritual fulfilment or enlightenment.* Both are different expressions of the same energy flow, and both will make you more time-heavy. I call this phenomenon the hungry mind; we have all experienced this craving for another book, or a new car, or a better home, convinced that this very latest acquisition will be all we need to make us happy, to provide the key to fulfilment or any other ambition we have set ourselves in time.

This idea – that a desire for enlightenment and a desire to be a millionaire are not qualitatively different – may seem shocking to you, but that may be because you have a value system that rates the pursuit of money as bad, and the pursuit of God as good, without seeing that the pursuit in and of itself is the problem. Any pursuit involves a "you" at a certain point in space and time who seeks something else imagined as better, which is a projection from the Past time-body.

You can get a good idea of a person's current state by that which he or she imagines as the state of enlightenment: if a person views it as a state of constant happiness, the person is unhappy, if another sees it as a state of peace, then that person is in turmoil. The truth is that the future holds nothing better than what you have right now. In fact, the idea of the future is merely a mental projection. There is nothing you can add to your life that would make you more complete than you already are; on the contrary, it is purely the pursuit of that "better" state that is making you unhappy.

Seeing that on its own is not enough. The Past time-body will continue to pulse through to the Present center as long as it has unfinished business. You cannot re-enact previous experiences in order finally to understand them, as the circumstances will have changed and the players in the original drama may even be dead. However, you can become conscious of those vibrations of experience through forgiveness and understanding. Both skills require seeing the situation in its totality – the people involved and the circumstance in which they all found themselves. This might seem to be an impossible feat, but it can happen at a point of great stillness, when the three time-bodies coordinate. I shall be showing you how to do that in Part III, the *Time-Light* Program.

Chapter **Six**
Your Present Time-body

*Man has no Body distinct from his Soul for that call'd Body is
a portion of Soul discern'd by the five Senses, the chief inlets of
Soul in this age.*

William Blake

Before your body was conceived, you were purely Potential, a
unified field, or unknowing consciousness outside of time and
space. On the death of your body, you will be that center again,
although the Past time-body may continue to reverberate after the
body's death. The Present time-body grows as the body forms in the
womb and finally comes into the world with the body's birth. By this
time, the Present time-body is complete, and creates and supports
the world in space and time.

Although the sense of separation, division, and multiplicity seems
like the only reality, it is but one of three realities that make you
"you." The ultimate truth remains that you are an undivided field,
which supports all life and is all life. That is your true home when
time and space collapse with the death of the body.

The final twist is that the "you" that is the universe is not that
which you may believe yourself to be. It is an impersonal you that
also shines out from the eyes of everyone around you. It is the
unified field made separate and individual, a multiple expression of
unity. The fact that your parents were already experiencing the world
as time and space before you were born suggests that they and you,
as bodies and brains, are part of this impersonal field.

In the first few months of life, when you were living largely from
the Potential and Present centers, you were extremely *Time-Light*.
The Past time-body has not properly formed since the newborn has

had few experiences that have not been fully witnessed or understood, other than the trauma of birth. That first experience leaves an energy pattern forming the skeleton that will allow the Past time-body to develop. Experiences that are neutral or do not engage the entity of past sadness or hurts do not leave an imprint in the Past time-body.

Child-development experts say that in the first few days and weeks, a newborn is unable to differentiate between itself and a world outside. While the child lives in the Potential center, there is no division. Philosophers say something similar: a baby and indeed a very young child cannot comprehend that there are "other minds" in the world besides its own.

The Present becomes the dominant pulse only when the baby has a physical need, and the first schism arises when the world does not satisfy it – when the mother is unable to feed the child or its cries go unanswered. This creates an energy print of upset or concern: it is a new pattern for the baby, and it becomes an early expression of the Past center. An energetic entity of sadness is being formed. Apart from the primitive energy pattern created with the trauma of birth, fear and a lack of satisfaction are invariably one of the first experiences that the Present center is unable to fully understand. This incomplete experience – seen from your own limited perspective – begins to form in the Past time-body. The origins of the Past time-body are therefore pain, fear, and hurt; the child becomes the adult who spends the rest of his life running from those earliest and primitive emotions in search of pleasure and gratification. From these feelings the child also has the first intimations that it may be different, and separate, from the world.

The Present time-body has a memory, but it is simple in comparison to that of the Past. Its needs and desires primarily consist of food, shelter, warmth, and other bodily needs, including sex, and so any emotion associated with these leaves its own imprint. They usually revolve around sensations of fear and pleasure: one is to be avoided, the other to be pursued.

Simple memories such as these have reverberations in the Past time-body. As we shall see in the next chapter, most events that are not neutral are extended, shaped, and given a meaning in the Past time-body until the energetic imprint of the experience becomes a model of reality. One bad experience of x is extended in time until we have our model that tells us something about the world out there: that all xs are always bad.

Most of us generalize from a bad experience to some greater or lesser extent. This tendency is the bedrock of prejudice. One day you are mugged by a shaven-headed youth in Detroit; from that you create a model of reality that all shaven-headed youths are violent, or that Detroit is a violent city. If you get food poisoning after eating a meal at a local restaurant, your model of the world tells you that the restaurant is to be avoided because it serves poisonous food.

Models of reality are not always *wrong*; they are based on sense data, after all, even though it may be partial or incomplete. These models are, however, invariably *not true*, because they are a description, a past impression imposed on the changing present moment.

If we were able to live entirely in the Present, we would see every experience as new and different, which of course it is. As such, we would *respond* to a situation – the appropriate method of meeting any experience – instead of *reacting* to it, which we do when we live from the Psychological past.

The drive of all Three Selves is towards greater understanding. For the Present, this is mainly achieved through the sciences as it attempts to explain the world and the universe. Nevertheless, the sciences explain only the Present center, the world of phenomena, which can be named, categorized and measured, or theoretically demonstrated through mathematics. As the sciences are derived from the same time-and-space continuum that they explore, scientists often fail to see their limitation, as they and their tools are part of that which they measure and analyze.

As there is no apparent evidence of God in the Present, the sciences therefore proclaim that there is no God, but that is only one-third of the story. God as a first causal agent – the first observer, if you like – would be outside of the time and space that it has created, and so scientists within time and space would not have the capability to know God.

The world as facts

In reality, in the here and now, there are no problems. There are only facts. It is a fact there is a war; it is a fact that children are starving in Africa. As such, the Present responds to a situation; it is the appropriate method of meeting any experience. In Part III, you will discover in the *Time-Light* Program that there are only two things you can do with a fact: either you act on it or you are unable to do anything, because it is outside of your powers to do so. A problem, on the other hand, is a loop system that has no resolution, and instead creates a pattern of worry, as happens with the constant iteration of the pulses from the Psychological Past. It is also the beginnings of depression as the rational mind seeks to find an answer – and cannot.

The conceptual brain

The Present time-body also includes the brain, with all its neural firings and its hemispheric interplays. The main *modus operandi* of the brain's thought processes are the use of concepts, a remarkable intellectual leap that appears to separate us from all the other animals of the earth in terms of complexity. With a conceptual mind, we conjure up dimensional models that allow us to build a world of houses, temples, roads, bridges, vehicles, ships, planes and space rockets.

However, the conceptual mind is a false friend. Although it allows us to build a world, it also separates us from a direct experience of being. The word "flower," for example, stands in the way of the thing itself. We satisfy ourselves by living second-hand lives at one remove from being, and we are content to experience life through words, symbols, images, and equations. We have become so hypnotized by them that we study the finger that points at the moon and no longer see the moon itself. While we are satisfied with a name for a description of the strangeness of things, we live a superficial life.

The conceptual also separates things into discrete bundles, and we see this demonstrated in virtually every human activity, from the sciences, medicine, technology to education. The reality is otherwise: things are indescribable and they are part of a whole.

Concepts also make tangible any feelings that are inchoate or have an undefined reverberation. Almost every thought and emotion you have is reliant on a concept, including the endless internal monologue and chatter that accompanies almost every waking moment, as well as your assumptions, your beliefs – your entire frame of reference about the world "out there."

The actualizing machine
Such is the power of the Present time-body when it joins with the creative energies of the Past and the Potential centers that the combination becomes an actualizing machine. Every thought that you think is true about yourself eventually appears in the world. If you convinced yourself – no doubt through criticism from others –

that you are poor at maths, you will demonstrate that "truth" about yourself in the world by failing at maths. If parents aren't up to the task, schools are excellent places where these feelings of lack, which last a lifetime, begin.

The philosopher Sam Keen once gave a good example of the processes of the actualizing machine. Throughout his formative years, his parents told him he was useless at mechanical things. He could not fix anything, his parents regularly reminded him, and of course so it proved to be. However, as an adult, he took a test with all the usual pressures removed – and he recorded one of the highest possible scores for mechanical ability. His innate skills made him a mechanical genius, but the actualizing machine of the brain had put him at the bottom of the class.

The world is made real by our imprinting of time and space, and the internal monologue and your emotional responses are made tangible by the conceptual mind. By definition, every concept is but a representation, and yet it is often more real to us than even the ground we walk on, so close is our internal world to us. Our concepts run deep; it is a concept that there is time and space, it is a concept that there is a world that is separate and "out there," the idea that your happiness will be found in that world is a concept; even the idea that you have a body is a concept! Of course, the belief that "you" are a body is a pivotal concept because everything else rests on it, from your own sense of identity to your place in the world and your relationship to it. A concept may be a useful form of shorthand that allows you to navigate in the world, but in so doing you have replaced reality – the immediate experience – with the conceptual description.

One of the principal tenets of Buddhism is that we must rid ourselves of the conceptual mind, so let's see how Buddhism would disabuse us of the concept that we have a body. In endeavoring to demonstrate that you have one, you might first point to some vague area around your chest or point at your head. No, says our Buddhist, that is your chest or your head. Where is your body? So you do a giant circle that encompasses everything: the head, the feet, the arms, the chest, and so on.

Therefore, says the Buddhist, you are telling me the body is everything. Let me make a list, and he proceeds to do so as if he were an auditor marking off the assets at the year-end. That is eight fingers, two thumbs, two arms, two eyes, two ears, one head, two knees, and so on. The body equals (which means it is the exact same as) all these individual items.

Three months later and you phone the Buddhist auditor with the sad news that you have had an accident. In an unfortunate grass-cutting incident, you have lost a finger. The Buddhist sympathizes and tells you you've lost more than a finger – you've lost your whole body. How can that be, you ask? Because eight fingers were part of the sum total of all the parts that exactly equated to "the body," he said, and now that you have seven, the whole sum collapses.

This sounds like a clever party trick. It also happens to be true. The body is nothing more than a concept, a descriptive shorthand that makes everyday life possible.

Chapter **Seven**
Your Past Time-body

The degree of one's emotions varies inversely with one's knowledge of the facts.

Bertrand Russell

Why do you think, and why do emotions suddenly well up? Moreover, what in you creates the constant thoughts – the "chattering monkey," as some Eastern religions call it – that accompanies your almost every waking moment and often in your dreams? These thoughts are not problem solving; they are the inconsequential mental mutterings that take on enormous significance, giving substance to this sense of "me."

Because we are doing it all the time, and we are often unaware of the process, it is not apparent how it happens, or indeed why. If you were to observe the phenomenon, you would see that it is a movement of time – from the past to the present, often to some imagined future.

Without the past, you would not have the narrator, the constant chattering companion for every experience. The narrator's nourishment is past experience, and it is the brain in the Present self that latches onto the energetic pulses from the Past and turns them into thoughts or a feeling. Every thought begins as a pulse from the Past self, but it happens instantaneously, and it is almost impossible to see this happening. However, once it has begun, it becomes a symbiotic dance between the Present and the Past. Thoughts from the present then create more pulses from the Past, back and forth, in a flow that seems to be endless.

As the dance continues through the years, so the sense of a substantial "you" builds and separates you from the world and from others. It is a dead-end. Eventually, we feel completely isolated and cut off from the world. This anguish is the beginning of depression, anxiety and a sense of despair and pointlessness, and the starting point for addictive behavior.

It is astonishing to realize that the two greatest psychological or spiritual crises of modern times – depression and addiction – have the exact same roots.

Some basic emotions arise from the Present time-body, but most begin as a pulse from the Past time-body, and the conceptual brain gives them substance. If concepts did not immediately arise, there would be just the pulse, which would dissipate without the fuel injection of concepts and emotions. The Present self has its own emotions, such as anger, fear, and disgust, but these are immediate responses to something in the moment. Once the danger or object of disgust has passed, so too does the accompanying emotion. It is only if you are not fully conscious in that moment that the emotion will form an energy print in the Past and eventually regenerate.

Experiences have different granulations. You could not compare an event such as going to your favorite coffee shop or fixing a chair with the death of your spouse and conclude that they were similar. They form different memories, and they are captured in one of the Past self's three energetic layers:

The Knowledge past: This is where the conceptual brain in the Present time-body and the Past work together in order to solve a problem, such as how to fix a fuse, understand a situation in the Present, or remember where someone lives or where you parked your car.

The Narrative past: These pulses, the ones that invariably create the "chattering monkey," tell you who you are in the world: the picture you build of your spouse, your cultural heritage, your position in the world. The Narrative is the Past time-body that also fuels inconsequential thoughts or a melody you cannot get out of your head. It gives you your sense of identity, a personality trait, or a series of beliefs from your upbringing and culture that tells you that you are a Christian, Muslim, or an atheist. Although its chatter is relatively harmless, it nevertheless provides a filter across the Present center that prevents it from having a direct experience of the here and now. The Narrative is not so harmless when it fuses with the hurts of the Psychological time-body. The mix is the origin of war, violence or terrorism. Our beliefs about religion, faith, or nationality become toxic when we add the chemicals of hurts, a sense of injustice or right. *The Psychological past*: This layer is made up of experiences we have not fully understood, from unresolved conflict, hurts, fears, and trauma, to moments of joy and ecstasy. It exists because we have not fully witnessed an experience – we have failed to fully understand or observe. We cannot understand an experience if we have been the central player and it has been seen entirely through our eyes, standpoint or needs. Furthermore, we have experienced it at a fixed point in space and time without being aware of the causal chain that led to it. When an experience is not fully witnessed, an energy print of hurt or fear is left in the Psychological past, and it will replay the event in the Present time-body – your day-to-day reality – in order to reach resolution and completion. It is a hopeless endeavor, however. As any action takes place only in the Present time-body, the people and the circumstances will inevitably have changed, as these are from a past that no longer exists. Receiving the pulses from the Psychological time-body, the brain's conceptual abilities can do only one of three things. It either begins creating a pattern in the world that is as close to the original situation as possible, or it creates a displacement, as I call it, where the feeling is similar – such as a sense of loss – but the player or circumstance is different. For example, if a sense of loss for a dead parent is projected onto someone living, the emotional response when that person goes away for any reason is disproportionate to the event. The third possibility is the creation of a mirror pattern, which is a reaction to an experience that is its complete opposite, such as an overwhelming desire for wealth based on a pulse from an earlier experience or fear of poverty. While there is nothing "wrong" in wanting to improve yourself and your lot, or in wishing for a better start for your children, a mirror pattern is all-consuming and can even be life-threatening, as happened to Charles Dickens, which we outlined in Chapter Two.

The woman who blew up the world

The past not only shapes our reality, it also shapes the world. Hanifah is a special Arabic name for a girl. It means "true believer," and it is a great honor and responsibility for all girls who are so named. An American Newsweek journalist interviewed Hanifah several years ago. Beautiful and intelligent, she had graduated with a degree in law five years before and now she was the mother of a darling daughter, aged one. Hanifah had recently celebrated her twenty-eighth birthday when she was interviewed on the eve of the "greatest day of my life," as she described it.

The following day she left her neighborhood in Palestine, passed through the heavily guarded border crossing into Israel, where she stopped for a moment, smiling at the young guard who seemed to like her, before heading to the school gymnasium, where she worked as a teacher's aid. Although she was a Palestinian Arab who prayed to Allah, Hanifah was liked and trusted by the staff and the children, and their friendship seemed to transcend the obvious differences of race, culture, and religion. This special relationship first alerted the terrorist cell to which her younger brother belonged. They approached her and asked if she was prepared to be a martyr, and kill the persecutors of her people. Without hesitation, she agreed.

So, on that very special day, after heading to the gymnasium, Hanifah detonated the bombs strapped around her body. She killed three children, and maimed five others in what was described as yet another terrorist outrage in the Middle East. "I want people to ask: Why? Why should a beautiful young girl, with everything to live for, who had a lovely baby daughter, why should she kill herself and the children in her care?" she told the journalist. "I want them to investigate, and find out how we live in Palestine, being bombed every day, losing our family, our children, our homes."

Hanifah's act of "terrorism" triggered a wave of missiles onto the poor homes of Palestine from Israeli encampments close to the border, an attack that was described on the news in the West that evening as "justified reprisals."

For Hanifah, the hurts that pulsed from her Psychological Past fused with the pulses from her Narrative to create a volatile mix. It is not unique; we all do this to some extent. Our thoughts loom over us in the present moment, and seem more real and substantial than the pavement beneath our feet. Our thoughts shape us. Our thoughts make a hell out of a heaven, and these thoughts – from experiences – make us ill. They can even kill us.

Beliefs shape the nation-state. Beliefs, as a group thought, set nation against nation.

Experiences that are not fully witnessed

What is an experience that has not been fully witnessed? It is one in which only "you" appear. You also fail to see the true nature of the other persons – and their true nature is as a Three-Selves being. Even a tragic and untimely death is not understood until we see the true nature of the dead person. When we do, we realize that just the Present time-body has gone.

A partially experienced event involves just you when, in fact, there are at least two players, plus the context of the circumstances surrounding the experience. You cannot understand anything if you see it only from your own perspective, which is held by a wounded, self-protective entity incapable of truly understanding any event. You also bring your assumptions, prejudices, and beliefs to every situation, and these, too, are the creation of partially seen and understood previous experiences. In essence, you have failed to gain sufficient altitude over a situation, and as a result, it has not been fully witnessed.

In my own case (you can read my full story in the box on p 78), I had a miserable childhood because of the wretched way my father behaved towards me. He would not acknowledge me and for the first seven years of my life only whistled at me when he wanted my attention. I could not understand this bizarre behavior and, of course, it left an emotional scar. Without the support and approval of my father, I was unable properly to function in the world as a young adult. I could not apply for promotion for a new position, for example, because I did not think I would be good enough. I could not even bring myself to go into a clothes shop to buy a shirt because I did not think I was deserving.

It started to make sense only when I was an adult on one afternoon when my parents revealed something very private about their marriage. In that moment, all sorts of experiences I had had as a child started to make sense. *I saw events outside of my own perspective*. It wasn't about me. It never was. Everything fell into place: I knew then – and completely – why my father behaved in the way he did. Yes, it was infantile and petty, but it was understandable. The understanding was a salve; but more than that, the weight was lifted. This realization was the beginning, not the end. I still needed my partner, Lynne, to point out when I was being unconscious to the movements from the Past time-body, and this continued to happen occasionally, until I could see the pattern for myself. It worked both ways: I was able to help Lynne see patterns in her life, too.

The boy who was whistled at
This is my story. I hope to hear yours when we meet.

My father was already well into his 40s when I was born. His marriage to my mother had been his second, and, if truth be told, he married her primarily because he needed a carer for his two sons from his first marriage, which had ended in acrimonious divorce (and in an era when it was much more likely for the father to gain custody of the children).

My birth, some six years after my father and mother married, was something that my mother truly wanted, but which my father saw only as a necessary part of the marital contract: you look after my two sons, and you can have a child yourself.

My father resented my arrival. Until the age of seven, he never called me by my name, but instead whistled if he wanted me. He never hit me and was not physically abusive, but he would constantly belittle and demean me. My mother told me that, when I was three, for example, I picked up a piece of trash when we were walking together in the park. "Put it in the receptacle," he said to me. When I didn't understand what he meant, he started screaming at me, telling me how stupid I was.

I vividly remember lying in bed in the morning, just waiting for the slam of the front door as he left for work. After that, I felt free – until he came home, that is. His return was never pleasant, and it was worse after he had been drinking, when he would pick a fight or find any small thing to criticize about my mother or me.

Although I was aware of just how hateful he had been, I was not fully conscious of how his behavior had affected me. I was not confident in the world and did not think I was worthy. I even found it difficult, if not impossible, to buy clothes for myself.

I married young – when I was 21 – and my first wife's birthday was the same as that of my mother! Although I was conscious enough not to be abusive – I hated my father at that time – I was nonetheless in a repeat pattern. I also developed a mirror pattern: although my father constantly told me that I was stupid and inadequate, I developed a sense of great pride, that somehow I was special and different. Pride is a complex mix of pulses and conceptual overlays, and is one of the more powerful forces that stand between you and a miraculous life.

All of that ended only when I had had enough, and decided I wanted to live fully and properly. I left my wife and met Lynne, who played an active part in helping me to become fully conscious of my past. Hating would not change the pattern, nor would an intellectual understanding – I had achieved both of those. I had to completely understand why my father did what he did, understand his own suffering, and realize that nobody is born a monster, but only becomes so. I had to feel his hurts and the reasons why he did what he did. Forgiveness means a 360-degree view of the circumstance. In that moment, I saw the situation in its totality – my parents, the circumstances, and me; in that moment, my three centers were coordinated. I was fully conscious. I saw my father as he truly was – a hurt child who had never been appreciated or loved. I had become part of his pattern, a victim of the energy flashes from his pulsating Past time-body.

In that forgiveness, I was able to let my father go, and I became healthy and whole.

That, for me, is the essence of a wonderful relationship: where either partner helps the other to become conscious. Most people marry and believe that is the end point, that life is already complete. Marriage and partnerships provide situations for growing and becoming conscious. As most people don't see that, they end up rowing and, eventually, divorcing from a sense of bitter disappointment or resentment.

Neutral and ecstatic experiences and addiction

Not all experience results in a feeling of sadness, hurt, or resentment. Much of it is neutral, but sometimes the experience is ecstatic, an oceanic feeling of unity or great joy. We do not understand these heightened experiences any more than we know why we feel sad or hurt. We do not know that they are the pulses from the Potential center. However, once the feeling passes, the basic movement of the pulses from the Psychological past to the Present is the same: we want to repeat the experience in order to understand it. The difference with an ecstatic feeling is that we endeavor to engineer the recurrence of the feeling by replicating, as closely as possible, the circumstances that led to the oceanic uprush.

This is the seed of addictive behavior. Whatever was happening at the time of the joyful surge of feeling – whether it was sex, drink or driving a fast sports car, perhaps – may become the subject of the addiction; we strive to have the experience again and so we repeat the activity that we associate with the feeling, *because we want to understand – to know where it came from.*

In one or more areas of our lives, most of us lie somewhere along the spectrum of addictive behavior. We may engage in a habitual pattern, a mild addiction, or a behavior so destructive that it wrecks our life and that of others. We are addicted because of the pulses, on constant replay, that come from the Past time-body.

The sudden feeling of joy, completeness, or unity is our natural state, and it emanates from the Potential center. It can happen suddenly and without our seeking it; in fact, it is most likely to happen when the Past time-body is quiet. When it does we often make a wrong association between the feeling and whatever we are doing at the time; we believe there is a direct cause-effect between that which we are doing and the sudden sense of joy.

This feeling of unity and completeness could happen, for example, while we are drinking a glass of wine. Because we do not understand the process or know of the existence of the Potential center, we somehow associate the feeling with the wine. This is an example of *associated addiction*, in which the sense of joy and completeness occurs unbidden and as if by accident while doing something else.

A *direct addiction* is experienced by drug addicts, for example, who are seeking out this feeling consciously through the use of cocaine, heroin or LSD. The drug addict ends his or her addiction only when he learns how to get in touch with the feeling of unity, love, and completeness naturally. The body also has a chemical addiction, and we look at this in more detail in the *Time-Light* program in Part III.

No matter its source, the feeling – and the desire to repeat the feeling – is the beginning of addiction. In a process that I call psychological witchcraft, the person with the associated addiction in particular replicates as best he can the circumstances from the original sensation in the hope of repeating it. As we have seen, the sense of unity actually happened because the Past time-body was quiet, thus allowing the pulses from the Potential center to dominate. However, these pulses are submerged by those from the Past time-body as it seeks to repeat the experience. Ironically, the more we want to replicate the experience, the more the pulses from the Past obscure the oceanic feeling from the Potential center. As a result, we try a little harder to have that experience again, so we take another glass of wine and then another, or we desire more sex, depending on the circumstances when the oceanic feeling occurred. Before long, we have become addicts.

The common view is that addiction originates from a place of great sadness. It doesn't. It comes from a fleeting sense of great joy and completeness. It also comes from a place of intelligence because it is seeking complete understanding. An alcoholic doesn't drink because he is unhappy; he drinks because he wants to be happy and whole again. An addict feels more acutely.

Understanding addiction in this way is the starting point to ending it. An addiction does not need to be suppressed or denied; it is an impulse that is trying to become conscious and understood. This is the beginning of intelligence and the end of addiction, a process that can be completed when you carry out the exercises in the *Time-Light* program in Part III.

The past in the present
Whereas addictive behavior is an active attempt to recreate the ecstatic moment, most movements from the Past time-body happen because something in life creates the circumstances that cause the past hurts to resurface. Of course, that "something," the event, is initiated by the actualizing brain via the pulses from the Past, but we are unconscious of that movement. It may be something that someone says or does or a situation that you witness. This happens to all of us from time to time – when our buttons get pushed, and the energetic entity is activated. It is, as we have seen, the past trying to reexperience itself. It is a moment of recognition as the past imprints itself on the present.

Invariably, the result is a reaction in the Present – a blind and involuntary response to a situation or experience. It is as though the brain is saying, "I know what's going to happen here." In a sense, it does. Although every experience in the Present is new and different, the pulses from the Past ensure that patterns are reestablished, and so a previous experience is reexperienced in the present. It could be likened to the points on a train track shifting and the train – your sense of a permanent self – being forced along a track that it has been down before instead of continuing a journey into new and unchartered territory. This pattern is on constant repeat, and it will come to the fore at any opportunity when an experience in the Present seems similar to an unresolved issue that exists as an energy imprint in your Psychological time-body.

The extension of experiences in time

The Psychological Past center "knows" the other two energy centers – it is aware of them both. The Present is a necessary expression of the Potential self in space and time, but its own needs are modest, if not basic, and it merely desires a sufficiency for its survival. It knows nothing of the Potential self.

The Past reflects both the glory of the Potential self and the primitive of the Present, and from that creates the sorrow and tensions of life. If we allow the Past center to dominate – and we do so by being unaware of its pulses that are translated by the brain – we never feel complete, never believe we have enough. The Present needs shelter: the Past desires a castle. The Present needs food: the Past yearns for a feast. The Present needs sex: the Past lusts after pornography.

The Present may have experiences – pleasurable and fearful – that are also extended in time. Experiences in the present cause sensations of pleasure, pain, or indifference – the latter happen with neutral experiences. Although these experiences are isolated, they are given substance in the Psychological past until they start to form our models of reality, so that one event becomes a truth that is so in every circumstance every time. We do this constantly while we are unconscious of the process. It is the birthplace of prejudice, opinions, and world views. A simple fear becomes morbid.

The Past is always an extension through time of our basic needs, driving the complex desires, fears and pleasures of the Present. In so doing, the Past creates psychological time, an energetic movement from a past and into a projected future. *That movement alone creates the imagined future, a fictitious place.*

And there will always be that ache, that lack of something

more that we just can't define. Most of us seek it in material rewards, but all the time, we somehow know the satisfaction will not last. We might look for it in sexual adventures, or in drink, or drugs or gambling, yet we know that we will crash down from the high or quickly bore of any new sexual thrill. Ultimately, a few of us look to fill that ache through religion and spirituality — but all the time it is the Past center striving for the very thing it cannot have. The only way "you" can get rid of the ache is to stop the process that is the ache itself – the Psychological Past, ever seeking to complete experiences it never understood. Only when that stops does the Potential center become dominant. That is the first and last freedom, the only freedom.

The birth of depression

Although all of us are influenced by the past, some of us are overwhelmed by the Past time-body. When this happens, the world gets too much for us. We lose sight of any worthwhile purpose to our life. Nothing pleases us, and nothing delights us. We also feel alienation – from the world, from others and even from our own body.

These are all symptoms of mild depression. It happens because we have become time-heavy. We have too much past, and it becomes the filter through which we see the world. As a result, we lose any perspective because we no longer have direct experience of the world around us. Instead, we see the past; worse, we *are* the past incarnate.

You could be walking through a beautiful park, but you are not present – you are thinking about your business problems. You could be playing with your child, but you are only going through the physical motions – you are worried about tomorrow's appointment with the doctor.

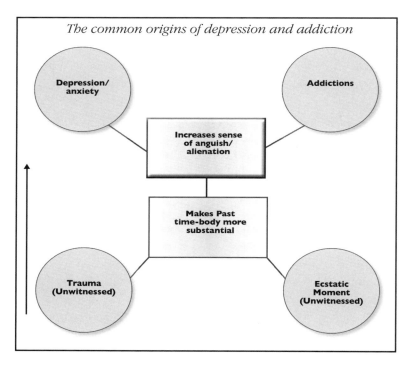

The common origins of depression and addiction

Depression/anxiety

Addictions

Increases sense of anguish/alienation

Makes Past time-body more substantial

Trauma (Unwitnessed)

Ecstatic Moment (Unwitnessed)

While the movement of the past happens to all of us some of the time, it becomes the entire life of the depressed person. The chatter from the Past time-body has become constant and even accompanies the person in his sleep. By this point, the person is haunted, and the Present has become shadowy. The Potential has all but disappeared.

Why has this happened? We have already seen that the Past time-body is seeking full understanding of experiences, and it does this in the only way it can – as pulses to the Present time-body. The Present is the only one of the Three Selves where experience happens because it is the only one in time and space. The Past seeks to have experience reenacted in order finally to complete the experience.

The pulses from the Past time-body therefore seek *an experiential solution, and not an intellectual one*. You cannot think or rationalize the completion of an experience – you must feel it – and totally. Understanding cannot be achieved through the intellect, paradoxical as that may initially sound. You could intellectually grasp that your mother always told you that you weren't good enough, but that doesn't make the hurt go away. You have to become conscious of those feelings in the Present in order to reach full and final understanding – and ultimately forgiveness.

The depressed person is endeavoring to achieve just that – a rational resolution to an irrational problem. Eventually, the past becomes an obsession as he tries to resolve problem after problem arising from the Past time-body. Yet the pulses from the Past are not "problems" *per se*, but incomplete experiences. It is a tragic and hopeless exercise. The past is just that; it cannot be recreated. People and the original circumstances have changed. So, the Present does the best it can, creating a close associative approximation and thus a pattern in your life, or a mirror reaction or displaced concept, where an unrelated person or situation becomes the subject of a previous experience.

The man who repeated himself

Bessel van der Kolk, a psychiatrist, originally handled the following case. Peter Levine later related it in his book *Waking the Tiger* (North Atlantic Books, 1997).

On one July 5ᵗʰ in the late 1980s, a man walked into a convenience store at 6.30 in the morning. He held his finger in his pocket in such a way as to simulate a gun.

As the store had only just opened, the cashier had only a few dollars in loose change to hand over.

Satisfied with his haul, the gunman left the store, and sat in his car until the police arrived. When they did, he got out of his car and with his finger in his pocket said that he had a gun and that everyone should stay away.

The police soon realized that the "gun" was a finger, and the man was arrested. At the police station, the officer in charge discovered that identical crimes had occurred on six previous occasions over the past 15 years, each happening at 6.30 in the morning on a July 5th.

The man said that he was a Vietnamese veteran, and the police realized that there was more to the crime than the usual hold-up. They took him to the nearby veterans' hospital to meet the resident psychiatrist, Dr Bessel van der Kolk.

The veteran told van der Kolk his story. When he was in Vietnam, the Viet Cong ambushed his platoon. Everyone other than him and his friend, Jim, had been killed. This tragic event happened on July 4th. As night fell, the rescue helicopters were unable to find them, and so the two spent a terrifying night, surrounded by the Viet Cong. At approximately 3.30 in the morning, Jim was picked off by a sniper and shot in the chest. He died three hours later — in the arms of the veteran — at 6.30 in the morning, on July 5th.

On his return to the States, the veteran reenacted the anniversary of his friend's death by holding staged holdups. As he explained, he did not hold one every year, because he was in jail the years that he missed. By staging the robberies, the veteran was recreating the fire fight, which escalated, just as it had in the past, whenever the police arrived.

In the wrong hands, the veteran may have been dismissed

as mad. Fortunately, van der Kolk was able to help the veteran see that he was acting out the past in order to resolve a deep emotional scar.

Using the Three Selves model, we see that the pulses from the Psychological Past were being interpreted and reenacted in the Present. The veteran was attempting to replicate the original situation in order to resolve it.

The story of you

We have looked at the influence of unresolved experiences that reside as energetic imprints in the Psychological Past, but what of the other two centers in the Past self? One's own story, as stored in the Narrative center, does not always lead us to war and conflict; it also provides the backdrop for our identity in the world. While it may be true that I am white and Anglo-Saxon, brought up in a democratic, Christian country, these truths are relatively so and have meaning only because others are not Christian, white, and Anglo-Saxon.

These facts about me – my story – are given depth, color and shading by my experiences until they become the truth by which I live and determine who "I" am. Through experience, my story creates a value system that determines the things with which I wish to identify, and those I don't. Once established, my story then presents itself to the world in what we might call a personality, although it is certainly not a consistent self. No personality remains the same all the time, because there are always various forces at play. Nevertheless, there is a persistency of type made up by characteristics that developed with our earliest experiences but that have been either amplified or suppressed by experience, culture, and upbringing. That is why we sometimes do something "out of character" – a wonderful expression that illustrates the play-acting nature of our story – and suddenly lose our temper or become moody or violent.

The constant chatter, the non-stop monologue that accompanies our every step, also adds potency to a sense of self by way of the Narrative time-body. Almost from the moment we wake up and until we sleep – and often while we sleep – our narrative, our personal back story, keeps up an inconsequential commentary of everything that is happening around us. And as if to keep us entertained, it even sometimes provides some music to accompany the commentary. Our narrative is also where the music loops live; that snatch of music you heard on the radio this morning is repeatedly played in your mind until something else replaces it.

You in the world
Another layer of the past also helps to create the sense of "you." The Knowledge past is the storehouse for everything you know or have learned about yourself and the world. Personal knowledge adds color to the "you"; because of it, you know where you live, whether you are married and have children, where you work, and what you do there. It also stores impersonal knowledge, which helps us function in the world, although generally this type of information is less important than personal knowledge. It is more important that I know where my home is, for instance, than whether I can point to Kenya on a map. Nevertheless, together they help fuel the narrative, your story.

And so it is that the three layers of the Past time-body flow back and forth with the Present and its conceptual brain, creating the sense of a solid, never-changing and continuous self. Increasingly, this sense of self develops more time and space between it and the world. Eventually, many of us suffer from the great disease of the West –

isolation, depression and even despair.

Although it feels very real, the sense of a permanent self is a fiction, created by energetic pulses – but a mightily powerful one. Our internal monologue overshadows our experiences, dwarfing everything and everyone else. We are in a prison of our own thinking, and it is so persuasive that we have convinced ourselves that it must be the truth. Our thoughts are like giants that loom over everything, separating us from others and the world.

Chapter **Eight**
The Potential Self

*Unity can only be manifested by the Binary. Unity itself and
the idea of unity are already two.*

The Buddha

Your happiness depends on the degree to which your Potential
center is prominent – how much its pulses are allowed to make you
"you" at any time. When – or if – that happens, you have an
unshakeable sense of coming home, of being connected to
everything and everyone. Fears dissolve, and your sense of isolation
and separation is replaced by love and a sense of unity.

Although this is your ultimate birthright, it is possibly nothing more
than a fleeting sense right now, and so we grasp for it as best we can
through the pursuit of material gain and success in the world. This
sense of happiness is a pale shadow of the joy and sense of unity from
the Potential center. Without it, we attempt to realize happiness. As
we become time-heavy, we develop a sense of a substantial self that is
separate from the world. This self then needs to go out into the world
in an attempt to discover happiness.

Yet, the "you" that desires happiness is nothing more than a
thought form, created from sensations of pain and pleasure, and the
many fugue-like variations on the theme. The "me" is given meaning
and substance with the aid of narratives and belief systems that, in
turn, create concepts through which we see and interpret the world.

These thoughts also determine the world in which you live and the
boundaries you see in front of you. If you live by the belief system that
tells you money does not grow on trees, you will always have
problems with money in your life. If you believe that the world is

hostile – and this is a vitally important issue to examine in yourself – then people will not be friendly, and situations will invariably turn against you.

How can thinking be so powerful? On its own, it cannot. However, it is your third center – the Potential – that gives these thoughts power. The sense of unity and love comes from the pulses of the Potential center, but it is also the field of all possibility, the creative source that will make real anything on which you focus.

The Potential center has been known by a variety of names by different cultures through the ages: consciousness, Atman, Nirvana, Mind, Krishna consciousness, the ground of being, the collective unconscious, the Field and God, amongst others. Whatever its name, it is consciousness, or the Potential center itself, that makes all of life possible.

The creative power of the Potential center is that which thinkers of the New Age refer to as The Secret, the Power of Attraction or manifestation. As described, it is a simplistic idea – that it is possible to think happy thoughts and have a million dollars mysteriously appear in your bank account. Invariably our wishes come from a place of unhappiness and dissatisfaction. So long as we are unaware of the processes of psychological time, it is more likely that our ambitions and hopes are coming from the Past time-body as a reaction to a hurt or sadness. There is no clarity when the three centers are each sending pulses, when we do not know which time-body is the dominant self, or when we are imagining a better future from a disappointing past. Only when these issues have been understood can we hope to harness the power of the Potential center properly. Paradoxically, when we do we want nothing else!

Our attempts to grasp just what the Potential self is can be likened to a goldfish swimming around in its bowl and wondering what water is. However, unlike water that was put in the bowl by an outside agency, there is a paradox at the heart of the Potential self: it is its own creator. It perceives itself into being and, in the perception, shifts from a field of potential and unity into a world of matter, multiplicity, and separate forms. It is the supreme observer, whose observations bring you, as a body and brain, into being.

The you that isn't there
This is not "my" consciousness at all, but the universal consciousness made subjective. The Potential self is not matter, but it manifests matter through the act of perception. It is outside of time and space, but creates both dimensions through the Present time-body. As such, your body is a space-time suit within its own creation, strange as that sounds.

The extraordinary truth is that you are a miracle because you are the eternal expressed in time, and the infinite appearing in space. Even this is not quite true – because there is no "you" at all. There is the Potential self, which finds expression through a body that you mistakenly call "me". There is no-space and no-time behind time and space. There is no-body behind you. When the Indian sage Ramana Maharshi was dying from throat cancer, his dedicated followers were beside themselves with grief, imploring him not to leave them. A little puzzled, Maharshi asked his adherents where they thought he would be going, as there was nowhere he could possibly go. On his death, and on yours, the space-time continuum collapses, but you – as the Potential center – go nowhere, because, without space, there is nowhere you can go.

When mystics say that you are not a body, they mean that you are the Potential center, the unified field that has no separation or division, but only the appearance of such. Although you are fully ensnared in the drama of life, it is just the Potential self unfolding. It is even a mistake to say it is all you – because there is no "you" or indeed me, either.

Your body will die, and the graveyards are full of evidence of that; the Past, in time, will also die, but the Potential never dies, because it was never born, and the two events of birth and death happen in time. A body also moves in space, and the Past time-body travels with it, but there is no movement in the Potential self. The ultimate truth is that you were not born so you will not die, and although the drama of life appears to be going on, nothing is actually happening.

Although that is the absolute truth, an attraction between the Potential, or consciousness, and a body does take place; without it, the curtains could not go up, the lights would not dim and the drama would never begin. And just as we become lost in a great film or compelling play, so we quickly forget that we are also the Potential self, and we begin to identify solely with the body having its experiences. This attraction explains why an inchoate sense of a "me" starts to form as the first sensations of pleasure and pain occur when we are infants, and a division between the world and myself starts to manifest.

However, the sense of a "me" as a feeling thing only truly develops with the rise of the Psychological Past center, the shadow self that sits between the Present and the Potential selves. This is the pull – and the tragedy – of the Past time-body. It knows the body just wants enough, but it also knows that the Potential self is everything; the Past time-body's only expression is to want more, a pale imitation of the completeness of the Potential center itself.

Only consciousness

Advaita is an esoteric branch of the Hindu faith. To its followers, it is the purest and truest expression of Hinduism and of all faiths. Its central philosophy also lies at the heart of Buddhism – Zen Buddhism in particular. Put simply, it states that there is only one thing in the universe: consciousness. There is no you, no me, nothing but one thing. Because there is only consciousness and no "me," even the idea of enlightenment is also an illusion because there is nobody to be enlightened.

However, although consciousness or the Potential center – the water in which the fish swims – is the absolute reality, just as important are the relative realities experienced by our Past and Present time-bodies. It is not enough just to be still and "be" the Potential self. If you want to live your life fully and to do so every day, you have to see with great clarity the complex interplay between the three centers and to observe which one is "talking" at any time. Each has its distinct pulse, and each will have its say, depending on the circumstances. One of the aims of this book is to help you identify each in turn. Sometimes several centers will try to speak at once, and, again, you need to differentiate and understand what is being said and by which center.

The Hannah filter
In the world of time and space, $1+1+1=3$. In the world of time and space, you have three centers. However, outside of this world, strange things start to happen to our mathematics: outside of time and space, $1+1+1 = 1$. At death and before birth, you are the Potential center, but from the perspective of time and space, this center is unknowable. More precisely, it is beyond our knowing because that which is in time and space cannot grasp that which is eternal and infinite. As your brain provides the framework for space and time, it cannot begin to understand something that is outside of both. If you try to imagine infinity, you will still see a wall. There will be a limit.

Outside of time and space, $1+1+1=1$, a phenomenon that I call the Hannah filter. It is named after the mother of Isaac Newton, the celebrated physicist best known for his work on gravitational influences, who also examined the composition of light. Between 1665 and 1666, Newton carried out a series of tests that he called *experimentum crucis* (crucial experiments); in them, he demonstrated that white light is made up from a spectrum of colors. From the one, many. From the unknowable one, multiple selves are created. Flip it around. Many also become one; the spectrum of colors collapses back into its originating single white light. Flip Hannah's name, and it still reads Hannah – it is the same thing, but read the other way round.

The Potential center is the ground of all being, the creative force of the universe, which makes life possible. For the Christian Kant, it is the noumenon, or thing-in-itself without multiplicity; to the Buddhist it is Mind; to the Hindu, consciousness or Atman; to the Jew, the I-am-that-I-am.

While it is unknowable to the rational mind, which can formulate merely a concept of the Potential center, it is something that is closer to you than even a thought. It is that which sees and hears, it is that which has been the constant observer while you are awake and when you sleep, from the moment of your birth – and before it, too. Your body ages, but this is ageless; it "feels" the same as it did when you were five years old. It is the "I am" that begins every existential statement you make: I am hungry, I am tired. Although the "I am" is never hungry or tired, it finds its expression through the body in time and space. In the stillness, you witness that which sees through your eyes, the consciousness that supports life and the room you are sitting in, the buzz of the fan, the birds singing outside, and the cars driving past.

It is clearly intelligent, but it also appears to be unknowing. It does not know itself. The only way a unified field could know itself is by creating itself as a multiple self. Therefore, your sense of "you" as an isolated and separate being is a necessary illusion; it is necessary because if, like Toto in the Wizard of Oz, you lifted the veil and saw the Wizard for what he truly is, the show would end. Perhaps you are not supposed to know that you are an expression of a unified field; perhaps, though, it is a process of returning home, but as a knowing and conscious being.

"You," as a sense of a separate self, come into being in relationship to the world and to others. The Potential and the Present centers not only combine to create a world in time and space, but also become knowable only in relationship to this world, which seems to be outside of us or, more precisely, outside of our body. Until we return home to the Potential center, we are deluded and bewitched by this relationship, this dance between the outer and the inner, a dance that is enriched by our internal monologue, the narrative of our life and the pulses from the Past. As I have said, our thoughts are like giants; they make our internal landscape seem more real than any external one. In this process, our sense of alienation increases, and we become convinced by the evidence of the senses that we are separate and alone. We are imprisoned within the cage of our body, sentenced to solitary confinement until the day we die – or until we awaken.

The move towards understanding
All of life is a movement towards understanding. That is why the Psychological Past constantly seeks to relive an experience in order to finally understand it and so put it to rest. That is also why the constant endeavor of humankind throughout time has been towards an understanding of its world, primarily through the sciences. Even the theory of evolution can be seen as an expression of understanding; yes, we seek to survive, and those of us who best adapt to our environment may be more likely to do so, but we have another thirst and hunger – for understanding

and knowledge. It is the one common factor that unites all of humanity across all time: we always seek to understand and to express our understanding, through the arts, mathematics, geometry and the written word – whether on a PC screen or a TV, on paper or parchment, on stone or on pyramids, or even on cave walls.

If the quest for greater understanding is indeed part of an evolutionary movement, the ultimate understanding that we are all expressions of the same unified field may be evolution's end.

Chapter **Nine**
Understanding the pulses

Home is where one starts from. As we grow older
the world becomes stranger, the pattern more complicated
Of dead and living

T S Eliot

It is extraordinary to realize that the sense you have of yourself as
a permanent self. is in fact nothing more – or less – than the
culmination of the pulses that emanate from one or more of your
centers. That is why you continually change. At any time, you are
the embodiment of the dominant pulse from any of the Three
Selves.

The voice – or pulse – of the Present is a quiet one, and we have
to learn to be more sensitive to hear it. It will tell you when you
need to eat – we all hear that one – and what it wants to eat.
Unfortunately, once the Psychological Past gets the message that
food is required, it often takes over, and its pulse will start
suggesting comfort foods that the body doesn't need – and that
may even prove damaging – but which it, as unfulfilled emotion,
desires. The Psychological time-body extends in time the basic
desires that come from the Present. This is often the reason why
people who constantly struggle with obesity find it almost
impossible to lose weight or to keep it off.

Love is a sense of unity
To take another example, love is the ultimate expression of the
Potential center, because true love is a sense of unity. How many
times have you been in love and felt that you were "lost" in the
other? This sense of unity extends beyond your lover and

includes the whole world and everyone in it. It will not last, however, because the Psychological time-body takes over with a myriad of thoughts and fears: This is magical, but how long will it go on? I want to repeat this feeling again and again. I do not want to lose this person.

Love, or the feeling of unity, is also timeless; being in love is a movement of the Psychological time-body and is in time – it asserts itself on the timeless. Eventually, this center's fears and worries will corrode even the feeling of being in love, and will put in its place a different energy that will eventually take the form of jealousy and insecurity but also care, tenderness and concern. The Psychological past time-body can have "good" emotions, too, but they are pale reflections of the Potential itself. And none of these emotions is love.

The Present may be in time, but it does not live in psychological time or create it; instead it merely provides the framework of space and time in which the drama of life may unfold. If the Present is threatened or frightened, it acts in the moment to protect itself. When the danger has passed, it ceases to concern itself with the problem. However, the experience leaves a resonance in the Psychological past, as we have seen, and a simple event is extended and made substantial. The basic sexual need is extended by the Psychological Past into lust or a craving for pornography, for example. It also begins to form your model of reality, so that one isolated event gets translated into a universal and eternal truth.

If the danger has a practical solution – such as fixing a broken stair – the Knowledge Past will solve it. However, if there is nothing you can do, such as when you might feel insulted, the Psychological Past often takes over. It may start chewing over the event that has passed, and seek revenge or find ways to avoid the danger in the future if you have been threatened. Either way, the experience lives on as a psychological reality, and the past event continues to have life, preventing you from being fully in the present moment.

When Jesus said that he, the Son, (the Present time-body) and the Father (the Potential center) were one, he had overcome the Psychological Past, as have all mystics throughout the ages. However, until we reach that understanding, each center has an important function to play, and together they make you what you are. The tragedy of life is that the Psychological Past holds sway – but it is a necessary tragedy. From all that we have discovered so far, the question that probably keeps arising is the most basic of them all: Why? If each of us is an individual expression of consciousness, of the Potential center, why should we go through this painful process of misidentification? Why can't we live simply in the miracle of the Present time-body? Why is the magnificence of the Potential hidden? Why, in short, are we living in hell when our birthright is heaven?

A return home
Throughout myth, there is the theme of homecoming, or *nostos*, a return to the place from where we started. References are found in books, poetry, and drama, but probably its best-known portrayal is in Homer's *Odyssey*, and it is as bittersweet a return for Odysseus, our everyman, as it is for the rest of us. In that sense, we can never go home again, because we have changed. As the poet T S Eliot put it in *The Four Quartets*, we return to the same place, but we know it for the first time.

When we were infants and in heaven because we experienced no separation from the world, we did not know we were in heaven, because we did not then know the hell of separation. If we are in a place and do not know it, it is of little value. In that sense, we are unconscious. Therefore, if our natural state is heaven, we must know when we are there, and the only way to reach heaven is to pass right through hell.

It is we who have to finish the Biblical myth of Adam and Eve. That is our quest – to return to the Garden of Eden as knowing beings who have tasted the fruit of the Tree of Knowledge of Good and Evil, who know it for what it is, and who have awakened from its hypnotic spell. Consciousness is a self-knowing process, and we play our part in creating a knowing universe. That's why each of the three centers is important – even the Psychological Past, as it plays a significant part in helping us to become conscious.

So how do we break the loop and have the experiential moment? This is the stuff of the *Time-Light* program, outlined in the next section. An important part of the process is true forgiveness. To see the totality of any experience is to forgive the situation itself and the players in it. The very seeing of something totally is the very act of forgiveness, and it naturally flows from that understanding. That forgiveness should be extended to you as well, because the idea of "me" is no more or less substantial than the concept of "others." In that moment of clarity, the narrative tape is wiped clean, and the concepts and beliefs supporting it crumble. This is possible only in moments of great stillness when the three time-bodies coordinate. You are fully conscious and because one of the centers is outside of time and space, even the past can be relived in vivid detail – and forgiven. From then on, every situation is vibrant, alive, and changing in a constant present moment, and nothing can be encapsulated within a concept – not even you.

True forgiveness
Although many in the New Age talk about forgiving, forgiveness

without understanding is hollow. If you forgive because you think it is the right thing to do (as you've been urged to do since childhood) rather than because you have a total understanding, you are still holding onto the resentment.

Those of us of a certain age remember the scene in the BBC TV adaptation of Evelyn Waugh's *Brideshead Revisited* when a drunken Sebastian Flyte vomits through the open window of Charles Rider's ground floor student rooms and contritely tells his new friend: "To understand all is to forgive all."

Whether he knew it or not, Sebastian was quoting an old French proverb, "Tout compendre c'est tout pardoner," and it has the ring of spiritual truth about it. Although we cannot know everything, we are able to use our own limited experience to empathize with the plight of another and so understand the situation. For the briefest of moments, we switch off the unconscious narrative in order to understand somebody else. In that moment of empathy, we are conscious.

The man who was able to forgive

John and Joyce live in upstate New York. They have one daughter, Jamie. When Jamie was seven, she heard the shattering news that she had failed her entrance exams to a new school. All her friends had passed. Devastated, she ran up to her room and collapsed on the bed. Her parents rushed up to the room and reassured her that it didn't matter, that it was just a silly exam.

"The unspoken issue was that she felt she was stupid. She had learning difficulties, and she knew she couldn't keep up with her friends in the classroom. But we never dealt with that, and it became the first lie between us. After that, it felt that there was a space between us and Jamie," John recalled.

But the problem went deeper. As a child, John had also experienced learning problems, and in the tough environment of his family, he was often reminded that he was "stupid." Although this all happened many years ago, the feelings were still raw, and John didn't know how to cope when he was confronted with the same problems with his own daughter.

Worse was to follow. Jamie became increasingly distant. By the time she was 13, John and Joyce started to suspect she was drinking. Again, it was something they didn't want to confront or deal with, and they hoped that somehow the problem would just go away. Again, it went deep for John, whose own father had been an alcoholic.

Eventually, Jamie moved on to drugs when she left home for university, and John and Joyce felt hopeless, shut out of their daughter's life.

Then, one day, Jamie was on the phone, sobbing, telling them that she had been raped. John and Joyce drove through the night and reached their daughter by the morning. "We couldn't believe what we saw. She was thin, she looked a mess, she didn't look like our daughter," said John.

John had seen enough. He knew he had to tackle his own demons if he was to win back his daughter. "We knew we had to do something, and we had received some counseling. I just instinctively knew that the only way out of this mess was forgiveness. I had to forgive myself, my parents, and Susie," he said.

His forgiveness was severely put to the test weeks later when Jamie was living with them again. Jamie gave him a note from her drug dealer. She had to pay up or she would be killed, the note said.

John went to meet the drug dealer with the money and a note of his own. In it he said that he knew the drug dealer was capable of better, that he knew he didn't want to hurt his daughter. He gave the note and the money to the dealer and left.

Two years later, in an Alcoholics' Anonymous meeting Jamie was attending, the drug dealer revealed that his life had changed the day a stranger had handed him a note.

Forgiveness saved the drug pusher, John, Joyce, and Jamie. It had wiped clean the past, and the patterns stopped. When John healed himself, he healed Jamie.

(From It Went Without Saying, *Troy Book Makers, 2010).*

The Sebastian Flyte moments are rare in our life. We spend much of our time oblivious to the processes that shape our life and our day-to-day sense of reality. It is as though we sleepwalk through the day, unaware of the chattering of the narrative, of the filter of the Past through which we see the world, of the concepts we live by that support the beliefs that translate our experiences. In turn, the narrative is created from experiences that are only partially observed.

A fully witnessed experience – one that is completely understood and observed – leaves no traces. When we are fully conscious, we not only see ourselves, but also the other people, the situation and the motivation that has created the experience. In that moment, we understand all and we forgive all.

As babies, we may not have understood that our mother didn't immediately tend to us at times because she was busy doing something else, not because she did not love us. However, because we did not have sufficient "height" above the situation, these became the very first experiences of ours that were not fully understood. From that moment on, we started developing a feeling of separation from the world, and that wonderful sense of unity and oneness – from the pulses from the Potential center – began to weaken.

Even so, the baby and the young child are still usually *Time-Light*, unless they have gone through a traumatic experience, and it is only with the passing years, when past experiences build and seek reiteration, that we become weighed down by time, until we see only the past and not the extraordinary "now" of being alive. Life becomes more difficult and less pleasurable until we feel separate or disconnected from the joy of living, which can be experienced only in the here and now. Most of us live through the there-and-then.

This movement from the Past center reinforces the sense of time, taking us away from our very first feelings of unity with the world and our association with the Potential center and toward the sense of a world that is "out there," completely separate from us and over which we have little influence. Nonetheless, out there is where we seek happiness, joy, and even spiritual fulfilment. We will never find it because the world out there is patterned by the past of unfinished business. We are like the dog that forever chases its own tail.

The Past time-body is therefore the source of the feelings that lie behind the concept that the world is separate from us, a sense that is subsequently reinforced by the sciences, which also work in a world that is separate from the scientist and us. These feelings inform us of our world and of who we are. Unobserved and undefined, they form our assumptions about a separate world, and they give life to the fiction of a self as permanent and fixed. These are "mega-feelings," as I call them, because they create the metaphysical backdrop to our lives.

Unity, the ego and enlightenment

Through the ages, religions and spiritual practices have

attempted to create unity in man, or unity between man and God (or the Potential center). Yoga, for example, actually means "unity," although the only yoga that seems to be practiced in the West these days is Hatha Yoga, the yoga of the body, which is merely a preparation for the main yogas. The four yogas of unity resonate with the world's main religions. Karma yoga, or the yoga of selfless action, has its reflection in Christianity; bhakti yoga, the yoga of devotion, has hallmarks of Islam; raja yoga, the yoga of concentration and meditation, shares similarities with Hinduism; and jnana yoga, the yoga of knowledge and discrimination, offers many of the practices of Buddhism and Judaism.

Many other practices claim to help you reach unity. Some focus on the Present time-body – through deprivation, starvation or physical austerity – or on the Psychological Past, often described as the ego. In the latter disciplines, you are encouraged to destroy the ego, or to stop thinking, through meditation and selfless acts. While you remain unconscious to the constant pulses from the Past center, you could no more stop thinking than you could stop breathing. Eventually you will start thinking that you have stopped thinking! What matters is to see thoughts for what they are, where they come from and what they signify. It is like watching clouds passing over the sun. You still know the sun is there, and you know the clouds will pass.

Spiritual practitioners and gurus offer rituals and practices to still the mind, through mantras or prayer. Stillness is vital if you are to fall back in love with your life, although deep stillness comes about not from rituals or mind-deadening mantras, but from clarity about all of thought's processes. It occurs naturally, as you begin to recognize the movements, or pulses, from the Psychological Past. That stillness is permanent, with a quality beyond anything achieved by ritual or even meditation.

It is also very important to understand the drive for enlightenment, liberation, or self-realization. Where does it come from, and what in us has that desire? The Present time-body has no need to be realized: it knows what it is. The Potential center does not need to be realized because it already is that. This drive comes only from the Psychological Past, from a desire to be more, to feel complete and fulfilled. It may envision the state of enlightenment as a place of permanent happiness; if it does, this impulse comes from its own unhappiness. If enlightenment is seen as a state of complete serenity, it comes from its sense of agitation. If it thinks enlightenment is a place of complete fulfilment, it comes from its own sense of dissatisfaction.

Any attempt to suppress thoughts, kill the ego or starve the body derives from a sense of great unhappiness, agitation, or dissatisfaction, all of which begin as pulses from the Past center, which get defined by the brain as thoughts, feelings and concepts. Desires for enlightenment and spiritual fulfilment are merely a continuation of those original feelings, which serves to strengthen the original thought further. The ego is a necessary sense of "I," born from the cumulative effect of three centers, so which ego exactly is to be destroyed? At the level of the Present time-body, the "I" thought is necessary for the body to be fed and sheltered. At the level of the Psychological Past, it is a vital part of the process of discovery. Consciousness, or the Potential center, is just that: I, the only I in the universe, the I-that-I-am of the Old Testament.

It is important to see that all these concepts – of enlightenment or spiritual fulfilment – are merely more thoughts. Without those thoughts, you would be happy, fulfilled and enlightened! The thought that you are not experiencing any of these states is the only thing that stops them from coming into being.

Nonetheless, you are dissatisfied with your life, you have fallen out of love with it, and it is perfectly sane and rational to want something better. So if it is true that any movement towards happiness or enlightenment is only strengthening its opposite – the current state – what can you do? The journey back, your *nostos*, begins by truly seeing.

Chapter **Ten**
Beyond Therapy

You could live in heaven, but you choose to live in hell. The only question you have to answer is: why have I made this choice?
Bryan Hubbard

What is the *Time-Light* program? Is it a philosophy, a therapy, a self-help method, a way to reach enlightenment, or perhaps just a discipline to overcome depression and addiction? In a sense, it is all these things and more; it is greater, and deeper, than the sum of its parts. It is a new way to see – yourself, the world, and the purpose of life.

It is a therapy because problems such as depression and addictions are impediments to "enlightenment" – shorthand for knowing that you are part of a unified field. But it's a therapy with a difference; it's not one of the "talking therapies", which have their place as a short-term coping mechanism, but which don't get to the heart of the problem. *Time-Light* is, instead, a "silence therapy" because problems are made real and given flesh only through definition.

It is a philosophy, but it has no value unless you are prepared to work with it in your everyday life. It is a self-help program, too, but it isn't designed to deliver the usual prizes of wealth, more sex, fame, and the rest (although it might give you those things if you really want them).

It's about you, in your life, right now. It tells you who you really are, and once you know that, everything else will follow. It tells you the truth about yourself before you die – so you can bring it into the world every day, which is your true purpose.

There's a wonderful story about the Buddha who spent a great deal of time deliberating about going out into the world following his own enlightenment. His fundamental message was – and is – "you" don't really exist! That which you think you are is a thought-form, a fiction. Even back in 500BC, the Buddha recognised this was not a great message to spread. The marketing boys would have a hard time putting a positive spin on that one.

If you examine most therapies, their underlying assumption is that there is a "you" that is the overlord, the commander that controls your thoughts – and is, essentially, "the real you". This commander also suppresses "bad" thoughts and emotions into a place called the sub-conscious. These bad thoughts are the suppressed side of yourself, pushed down into your psychological trash can.

One of the key messages of *Time-Light* is that the "commander" self – the supposed real you – is a fiction, along with all the other selves that emanate up from the three selves. There is no commander; instead, there is a continuous series of selves that take shape from the pulses that are always rising up to the Present time-body in order to be understood – not suppressed.

As such, emotions and thoughts are neither good nor bad. They are associated with experiences that are repeating in the Present time-body. They are not "you" any more than the "commander" self is you. These emotions and thoughts are ripples on the waters of consciousness. Not only are they not suppressed, they also do not need a psychological band-aid or positive thoughts or affirmations, either.

When a pulse rises to the Present time-body, emotions, thoughts and concepts almost instantaneously attach themselves to it, which gives the pulse definition and energy. This complex interplay of thought, emotion and concept is consolidated into a picture or image – that's how memory works. We visualize the past, and we see it as an image or a series of pictures. The process – from pulse to emotion/thought/concept to pictorial representation – fires the "negative" emotions that were associated with the original, and partially understood, experience. Anger, resentment, jealousy, hatred and fear aren't "you"; they are emotional associations with experiences that are repeating in the Present time-body. And they repeat because they want to be understood; they are seeking their own end.

"You" don't exist because the real you is everything, an expression of an eternal unified field. That's the good news, of course, but the Buddha feared he may have lost his audience by the time he got to that bit.

The other perplexing thing about *Time-Light* is how it came into being in the first place. As I mentioned, it was an immediate, and ready-formed, download. But what had triggered that? Was it the book I was reading at the time, or the years I had spent studying philosophy? Was it somehow linked to the mystical experiences I had as a small boy?

I don't entirely know, but once it had been created I wanted to test it with a series of questions. One question that many of us share is: why does there seem to be so much evil in the world? Why is there always a war going on somewhere? Then there are questions that you may have posed at some time: Why do we always want more when enough should be sufficient? Why do so many starve and a few have excess?

There's another question that I've toyed with over the years: Why is it that we don't "get" the religious truths? Since we were toddlers, we have been taught the sayings of Jesus, Mohammed, Krishna or Buddha but, for most of us, they just haven't made that much difference to our life. Even those of us who observe the religious rituals and forms aren't really transformed by the teachings, it seems.

There are only two possibilities here: Jesus, Buddha and the rest are mad, in which case we are right to ignore them, or we just don't understand what they are saying. Looking around, there seems to be a gulf between their vision of the world and the world as it appears to be for us. We are fed daily doses of news about muggings, murders, rapes and starving children and the saints are talking about a heaven on earth or a blissful state or nirvana. Looking at our own life, we seem to be making a mess of that, too. We might be divorced, or we have children we can't communicate with, or perhaps we have some addiction.

At the beginning, I asked the most fundamental question of them all: who am I? Although very few of us ask that question, it is the most important we can ever ask ourselves. I described it as the golden thread that would lead us to all the other answers.

I hope that I have demonstrated throughout this book that the Who am I? question is, indeed, the master question, and its answer supplies the answers to all our other questions about life, and our life, that we may have from time to time.

You are the amalgamation of three energy centers that become more substantial in time and with experiences, especially those that we do not fully understand. As such, understanding each center, its characteristics and functions will provide the answer to all of our questions.

There is evil in the world because we are more past than present and there is war when we fuse the Narrative past time-body and its sense of identity in the world with the hurts of the Psychological past time-body.

We make a mess of our lives because we live on permanent repeat as the Psychological past tries to reach a final understanding of a hurt or sadness.

And we don't get the religious truths because our Potential center has become obscured by the pulses from the Psychological past. As most of us live that way, we have created a world that is a hell on earth when it could be the heaven that our religious teachers promise us.

Spiritual truths are discovered only in life, in your life, and they are lived every day. The saint, guru or spiritual master who formulated the truths is at a different energy level to you. They are already *Time-Light* – and you are trying to understand what they say while you are time-heavy. They might as well be speaking a foreign language and, in a way, they are.

Because they have mastered themselves through time and you are burdened by time, you recognise nothing of what they say in your world. It doesn't make sense, and it doesn't even seem to be true. What could it mean to take no thought of tomorrow when you've got the mortgage to pay, or a child being bullied at school?

There is such a mismatch in the two visions of reality that, pretty quickly, you discard religion and spiritual teachings as so much wishful thinking or claptrap. Nonetheless, there will be times when you will reach out for a holy book, or even decide to pay a visit to the local church or temple. So what makes you do that if you have already decided it's meaningless? The same past-to-present movement that is messing up your life wants that mess – the misery or sadness – to stop. One remedy is the salve of religion and spirituality; another might be a car, or a new wife or husband. The ambition may change but the drive is always the same. It comes from sadness and regret – the yawning ache of despair at which we hardly dare look.

If we cannot achieve spiritual fulfillment from a book, what is the point of reading any book, including *Time-Light?* Books and words ready the mind much as a farmer tills the land in preparation for sowing – but true fulfillment is achieved only in action and in your day-to-day life.

The most important part of this book is not the theory, which we have now completed, but the experiential practice – that begins with the 21-day *Time-Light* program in the next section.

Are you ready to start the truly religious life?

PART **THREE**
THE 21-DAY TIME-LIGHT PROGRAM

That to which you do not fully attend will weigh you down

If you bring forth that which is within you,
Then that which is within you
Will be your salvation.
If you do not bring forth that which is within you,
Then that which is within you
Will destroy you.

The Gnostic Gospels

Please either prepare your own notebook or use the companion Work Book with this volume. The Work Book is a separate volume in which all the headings are in place, and the pages are laid out for your entries. All you need is a pencil. If you want to create your own Work Book, you will need to buy a lined note book of approximately 100 pages. Ideally, it should be 8 by 11 inches (A4 size in the UK) because you have some writing to do, although a notebook half that size is more portable. If you decide on a smaller format, you may need to double up on some of the pages, in which case you may want a notebook with approximately 150 pages. Use a pencil.

The purpose of these first exercises is to learn simply to observe the pulses from the three centers. Do not give them strength by thinking or by embellishing them with feelings or concepts. Without the momentum of the conceptual brain, the pulses will remain just that – and will dissipate. As the pulses from the Past center weaken, those from the Potential center will come through more clearly. You will realize that you are an expression of an eternal, unified field.

When you are doing this work, it is vital that you don't judge. There is nothing bad or evil about your thoughts or your unconscious tapes: they are as they are. Any judgment is just another thought form, and one that will send you right back to sleep. It is also important to do this work without expectation. Don't carry out the exercises in the hope you will get something out of this process – that you will become enlightened or be happy forever. Letting go of expectation is tough because your entire mental makeup is predicated on the concept of effort/reward in time. You do something because you want something else. This is another trap. If you expect a reward, you are projecting a thought-form into time: "If I do this today, I shall be enlightened tomorrow." Can you see that this very process is the problem? While ou are in psychological time, you cannot be in the here and now, and if you are not in the here and now, you are unconscious.

All of this seems difficult while you think about it – because your thoughts cannot know any different. It becomes simple and natural in the doing. What could be easier than to truly experience something with all your senses? What is so hard about writing down what you have just thought – and doing so without judgment? Is it really so impossible to change your tape and begin telling yourself something positive? Of course, you will become unconscious again, and the narrative will start playing – but then you will wake up and realize what you have been doing. Each time you wake up, you become a little more conscious, and that muscle will get a little stronger.

DAY I ▶ Just looking

▶This indicates the start of a new exercise, and one that you repeat every day until the end of the program. Although we will be adding a new exercise on each of the next 21 days, each day you will be repeating any exercise that has the ▶ symbol. This means that you will do the "Just Looking" exercise 21 times! It is a cumulative program, and you will be carrying out the best part of 21 exercises on the twenty-first and final day. Onerous as all this may sound, it is easy in practice. Each exercise will take only a few moments to perform.

If you are preparing your own notebook, put "Day 1" in the top lefthand corner of the page. Then write the word "Just Looking" in the middle. Always write in pencil.

None of us looks. We may look to cross the road or to see what is on the menu or to read our emails, but these are cursory forms of looking, just enough to get the required information. However, since the time when you were very young, you haven't really looked at anything purely out of fascination and curiosity.

By really looking, I mean absorbing yourself in something else with no thought of gain or power. Truly looking is the pure, undiluted act of observing without interpreting or imposing concepts. Once your conceptual mind has defined that which is being observed, you cease to look. If you really look at a flower, you see the utter mystery of it, and it is indeed mysterious when you get past the shorthand definition of "it's a flower,"

Therefore, our very first lesson on day one of our voyage to the miraculous is to relearn the ability to observe. I mentioned a flower as an example, so let's start with that (it could be anything, of course). Find time today to look at one flower in your backyard or garden; just one, but really, truly study it. Look at it for minutes, visually devour it, soak it in until the space between you and the flower disappears. Even though now that I've just told you it will happen, you will be waiting for "the moment" - but it will still happen. You will soon see that you have never really looked at a flower before.

You can do the same with your wife or husband. Really, really look at their face (it's probably a good idea to mention what you are about to do beforehand), and you will see things you had not noticed before. Truly! It will happen. Or over a meal, really taste the food in your mouth, its texture, its taste, its aroma.

In these moments when time itself seems to freeze, minor miracles may occur. "You," for instance, may disappear for a while into the face of your husband or wife, the taste of the strawberry in your mouth will be all that is in the universe for that short while. Better yet, thoughts of work, the new car, and so on will vanish – and you will see that you are perfectly at peace in that instant of complete absorption. In that moment, you will see with great clarity, without peering through a screen and filter. The Indian mystic and educator Jiddu Krishnamurti once said that all the misery in the world was in the space between the observer, you, and the subject, the thing you are looking at.

When you look at that flower, the space between you and it disappears, and with it all the potential for unhappiness and misery.

DAY 2 ▶ Thought-watching

If you are preparing your own notebook, on a new page write "Day 2" in the top lefthand corner. You need to split the page in two, so draw a line across. In the top half, write "Just looking" – because I want you to observe something different today – and in the bottom half, write "Thought-watching" because that is the new exercise we are carrying out today. Today's and yesterday's exercise have an arrow after them, which means it is an exercise that I want you to repeat every day for the remainder of the program.

The purpose of this endeavor is to get you back in touch with your natural inheritance and to fall back in love with your life. You have fallen out of love with your life because you are living unconsciously and according to a series of beliefs and concepts, fueled by a Past that seeks to relive experiences. Mega-feelings have created a series of foundation beliefs – these include a belief there's a world out there, that you're a separate being, and that you will find happiness or fulfilment in that world. You may have supporting beliefs that reinforce your world view: The world is hostile, it is every man for himself, money doesn't grow on trees, and he who dies with the most toys wins (rather than being the biggest baby, presumably). You may not be aware of these beliefs, and you might even deny them if you were challenged; nevertheless, the Past will invariably control the rational brain. Emotions always win out in a battle with logic.

We have seen how these beliefs have developed from experiences that occurred when you were not fully conscious, triggering an emotional narrative from the Past self that seeks completion. That narrative creates images that, in turn, have helped establish concepts that are invariably universalized so that "all x's are y."

Forgiveness is a natural endpoint of understanding, and in forgiveness concepts vanish, as an emotional journey from the Past reaches its final destination. However, forgiveness flows naturally from a complete understanding; it doesn't have to be forced. We have also glimpsed what it is like to live consciously, and the wonderful stillness and expansion of space that happens when you do.

That stillness happens when you are conscious – when the Potential center is allowed to become dominant and to co-ordinate with the two other time-bodies – but this sense of stillness is like a muscle. It needs to be frequently exercised, or you will fall back to sleep and become unconscious again. When you are unconscious, the pulses from the Past self start up again.

So we need to start exercising stillness. From today – and for the next twenty days – I want you to write down some thoughts and feelings you have or, more exactly, thoughts or feelings of which you are aware. Don't worry, you won't fill the notebook – you won't stay awake often enough to record each thought and feeling you have. This exercise is immensely subtle. As I have explained, an energy pulse that comes from one of the selves precedes every emotion and thought. Initially, you will not sense the pulse itself, but I want you to start waking up enough to the thoughts and the feelings that follow it. It's a little like catching wisps of smoke as the feelings scud across the Present center, and you have to be very still if you are to succeed.

In these initial stages, you may like to meditate first in preparation. If you already meditate, and you have a technique with which you are comfortable and familiar, stick with it.

If you are not a regular meditator, you might try a method that

I like. Begin by sitting comfortably in a chair. Make sure your back is straight and your feet are planted firmly on the ground. Rest your palms in your lap and close your eyes. Take a deep breath in, hold it for a few seconds, and then slowly release it. Breathe in and out slowly five times. Now move your attention to the tip of the nose until you feel it tingle. If you can't feel anything, don't worry. You just need to become a little more still, so carry on breathing deeply.

After a few more breaths, return your attention to the tip of your nose. Wait a few moments and you should start feeling it tingle. Now move to your toes, and again you should be able to feel a similar sensation. Repeat the process as you go around your body, to your fingers, your lips, your knees, your arms, and so on. Now just attend to the stillness itself. Thoughts may enter, but don't resist them. Let them pass over. Every so often, breathe deeply four or five times – and here's something else to remember: Smile. Not a manic grin, but just allow your mouth to turn up slightly. If you can maintain a degree of stillness, meditate for twenty minutes. If you start to feel uncomfortable or your mind becomes increasingly distracted, stop the meditation.

Now you may feel better able to watch your feelings and your thoughts. As you do so, just write them down, as a reporter would when writing the proceedings of a court case. It is important not to judge, criticize or condemn – those are also thoughts. It is not your job to discriminate between thoughts. A thought about God is not qualitatively better than a thought about a car; it is just another thought.

As you recognize this, you will see that the narrative from the Past gives thoughts a value or weighting. That is why "you" think one thought is more significant than another is. You will soon realize that you cannot hold the stillness for very long. As I say, stillness is a muscle that needs to be exercised, and in the early stages, you will be amazed just how quickly you lose attention and drift off back into the reverie of your narrative.

Take your log to bed with you. Just before sleep is a good time to record your feelings and thoughts. Leave the log by your bedside in case you awake in the night and want to write something down. The more you do this, the more this will happen. Remember, it is an internal audit – not a "things I did today" diary. It is there to record your interior landscape, and it is one of the first steps on the road to the miraculous life.

Day 3 ▶ Addictive behavior patterns

Write "Day 3" in the top lefthand corner of the page. Split the page into three. Write "Just Looking" in one section "Thought-watching" in another, and "Addictions" in the third. In a small subsection of the "Addictions" area, write: "What I did differently today." You'll soon need two pages per day.

From day 3, we're going to work on our addictive and habitual behavior patterns. All of the exercises outlined in this program work together, and by doing them every day you'll start noticing that you are becoming more conscious anyway. All unconscious behavior and patterns will start correcting themselves (and I'm using "unconscious" here to mean thoughts and feelings of which you have not been aware, not those that come from a subconscious or unconscious place). That is the key to everything we're doing – becoming *Time-light* is a self-correcting process, which unfolds naturally.

We are all addicts. Even if you do not drink, smoke, gamble, or have a sexual problem, you are still an addict. You are addicted to patterns of behavior as the past continues to replay itself through your present time-body. Eventually we become like a vinyl record, assuming you are old enough to appreciate the analogy, and the needle has created a groove in which it runs deeper and deeper. As a result, we keep on playing the same old tunes. The deeper the grooves become, the harder it becomes to move the needle onto a new track.

Sometimes we cannot do anything about our habitual behavior – we have to be at work at a set time, for instance – but most times, we can. When we become more conscious, we stop telling the same jokes, making the same remarks, and thinking the same thoughts.

Anything you try to change about yourself will fail or not sustain itself for more than an hour or two. That is because any effort with an end-point or aim in mind is yet another thought process; you are merely replacing an old pattern with a new one. In the world of time and space, all of thought is predicated on the assumptions that there is a world out there, that the world out there has a solution or an ultimate prize, and that through effort and time, we will attain that special prize. So, however you dress it up, or endow it with a quasi-spiritual name, it is the same process of effort ending in reward.

To break that mental habit, all we are going to do next in the program is observe and record – and, occasionally, say our observations aloud so that they lose any power they might otherwise have from being silently, or tacitly, permitted (as you will discover later in the program).

So, from day 3 onwards, we are going to observe and record habitual behavior patterns. They won't be hard to spot, because virtually everything we do, say, and think is habitual; while we remain unconscious to the movement from the Past to the Present time-body, we are the vehicle for the past, which is where habitual behavior lives. If you are conscious and present in the moment, you cannot have habitual behavioral patterns; when you are present, the past cannot be.

Right now, we are going through a program of waking up, which means that you are not fully conscious. You will keep "falling asleep" to the hypnotic drumbeat of the past, but, as I hope you are beginning to see, it's not important that you fall asleep again, but that you know when you have.

With this new exercise, as we attempt to observe our thoughts objectively, we will try to recognize patterns of the past. Every thought that is not problem solving is from the past.

However, I want you to do more than just observe and record. I want you to act. Every day I want you to do just one thing differently. It could be a minor change, such as buying a different newspaper, taking a slightly different route to work, having a filter coffee instead of a cappuccino, not putting butter on your toast, or going to bed at a slightly different time. The point is to do so consciously – and you record the fact in your log. You could even recite to yourself: I am doing this because I have consciously chosen to do so. It is important that you remember to do something different every day. Each time you do, you make those memory grooves a little less deep.

Most of us also have more serious addictions – ones that you would call a real addiction – but the process is often the same. In some types of addiction, especially with alcohol and drugs, there is usually a biochemical element, and this needs to be addressed separately (see Day 10). By now you know the rest of the process: addictions come from the Past self, and are often an attempt to recreate an ecstatic moment. It happens while you are having a cigarette, a glass of wine, or a cupcake, for instance. These associative thoughts – I had the ecstatic moment when I was once drinking a glass of wine – come about from a time when you were not fully conscious to the moment and so were not awake to all the implications. The Past has invested the thing with a quality that is fictitious but nonetheless convincing. For that moment, you genuinely believe that the glass of wine is somehow the cause of the moment of ecstasy. The same might go for cigarettes or some chemical enhancer. As a result, the Past develops cravings for a repeat of a pleasurable moment, which it believes is achieved if it repeats the action – such as smoking or drinking – taking place at the same time.

Because all this was going on while you were unconscious, a

behavior pattern established itself in the Past center. The wrong association was created. Had you been conscious at the time, you would have realized that the feeling of pleasure is, in fact, a sense of utter completeness, an at-oneness-with-everything that emanates from the Potential center. In that case, the cigarette or the glass of wine would not have taken the credit, and you would not have started to develop a craving and an addictive behavioral pattern that would continually seek to repeat the experience.

As you become more conscious, the sense of oneness will become more common and, because you are more conscious, you will not associate it with whatever you happen to be doing at the time. You may be drinking, you may be smoking when you experience this sense of oneness, but you would have experienced that feeling no matter what you were doing, and this you will see as the program develops.

Again, you will realize that the whole movement from the Past time-body is predicated on the assumption of a world "out there," and one that offers complete happiness or some ultimate prize. An addiction is merely a desire, based on a wrong association, which seeks to replicate a feeling of completeness, fulfilment, or happiness.

DAY 4 ▶ Thought-locating

You need to start a two-page spread each day from now on. Write "Day 4" in the top lefthand corner of the page. Now we need to create four sections across the two pages. Write: "Just looking" in one section, "Thought-watching" in another, "Addictions" in the third (with a small subsection of the "Addictions" area, entitled "What I did different today,") and now "Thought-locating" in the fourth section.

An energy pulse precedes every thought, but the movement is so subtle that it may take a while before you see this. Without interpretation by the brain, a pulse would not gain energy or definition, but instead would dissipate. However, while we are unconscious to the process, concepts, thoughts and past hurts quickly attach themselves to the pulses and give them life. Most people say it is the other way round, that thoughts spark feelings – and it is certainly the case that thoughts strengthen the feeling – but all the thoughts and emotions we have that make you a "you" as a thinking being begin with the pulse. Once that process has started, the emotions and thoughts act as a catalyst for more pulses.

After all, you had feelings, as does every newborn, long before you could think or formulate words and simple sentences. Eventually you learn to express that subtle pulse – sometimes it is a torrent or an uprush – and to put it into words. We have been doing this for so long now that we rarely notice that the words are a poor approximation of that feeling. We have just a handful of broad brushstroke phrases that are clumsy expressions of something so much more subtle, so quicksilver.

The exercise of keeping the log is the first stage in developing the ability to sense pulses without defining them as thoughts or emotions, to feel the pulse as it ebbs and flows. Disconnected from words, the pulse loses its potency because it is, quite literally, indefinite – it has not been defined. Ultimately, that which you do not define cannot sustain itself in space and time; deprived of its definition, it loses its energy.

As you become still, so you attend. However, just as a toothache disappears the moment you sit in the dentist's chair, so emotions and thoughts subside when you are watching and waiting in stillness. Eventually, you will fall asleep once again and the narrative will take over, but note each time it happens in your log.

For this exercise, I would like you to start calculating from which self the pulse comes. To begin with, it will be just a guessing game, but you will get better and better at it the more you do this exercise. The thought or feeling will rarely arise from just one time-body: it will be an admixture from more than one of the centers. The sudden thought of eating comes initially from the Present time-body as a pulse for food but is quickly embellished by the Past center as a need for comfort or reward food, such as a large slab of chocolate cake!

Here are a few parameters to help you gauge how the thought and feeling have come into being:

The Present time-body has basic needs for shelter, rest, safety, exercise, nutrition, and sex. It also has basic emotions that are directly associated with the body, such as fight or flight, and fear of an immediate danger. The brain is also a part of the body. It can solve problems, and it has the remarkable ability to think conceptually, which includes the imagining of things in space and time.

The Past time-body sits between the Present and Potential centers, and it can be pulled in either direction; it increasingly identifies with the drama of the world as its narrative begins to become dominant. Fundamentally, the Psychological past time-body is the Present time-body writ large. The Present center wants "enough" and sufficiency – it wants sufficient shelter, enough money with which to live, enough food. The Past wants more, much more than the body actually needs. This is because the drive for more is the only expression that approximates with the Potential center itself, which is infinite and eternal. While anger is an emotion from the Present time-body in response to an immediate threat or challenge, hatred derives from the Past center because it is a continuation of anger in time. The Present time-body may desire sex, but the Past self will experience lust, sexual deviancy, and even an interest in pornography, as these feelings are an extension of the basic sexual urge in time. The Present time-body may have a sudden feeling of fear, but it is in the Past self where you find phobias.

However, not all feelings are negative. The Past time-body is also capable of feelings of affection, kindness, care, concern, sympathy – and its highest attribute, empathy. Again, these are extensions in time of basic feelings registered in the Present self.

The Potential center, too, is part of the mix of "you." Like the Past time-body, the Potential center sits outside of time and space, but unlike the Past center, it does not reinforce the sense of time and space generated by the Present time-body. The highest expression of the Potential center is pure love, which is the sense of unity. Despite what most people think, hate is not the opposite of love, although feelings of hate do arise from a sense of disunity and separation. Love has no opposite – the closest negation is a lack of love, a sense of isolation and separation.

A feeling of completeness may come from the Potential center, but the Past time-body can subvert this into a great yearning. Similarly, the sense of unity can be translated by the Past self into a need for religion or contemplation. The Past time-body's feelings of general dissatisfaction and a need for more are not a reflection of the Present center, which wants just enough, but of the Potential itself, which is everything.

A quantum physicist might describe the Potential as the field of all possibilities. Because the Potential is not defined and not in space and time, it remains a potentiality in relationship to the physical world. It is important to grasp that the Potential is a creative force, a potential for every situation occurring in time and space. That is why thinking and feelings are so important; they act as a vital framework that gives shape to the creative power of the Potential.

Have some fun with this exercise and with the thousands of thoughts you have every day. You will not catch most of them as they fly across your mind, and most of the time you won't even notice you are thinking, but when you do become aware of a thought, try to figure out the center from where it has come.

You could even carry out this exercise retrospectively. Suppose that you were thinking this morning that you really didn't want to go to work today because you have that meeting to attend – which center would have such a thought? Or you really hope that some individual doesn't get into your train compartment – and that? I need to lose weight before the summer. . .my shoes are killing me. . .it's going to rain and I'm going to get soaked – how about those?

Working out where these thoughts come from is all part of becoming conscious, of slowing the narrative, of stopping the movement from the past to the present. All of thought is in psychological time, a movement from the past to some assumed future or to some imagined present. Carrying out this exercise correctly can be about becoming a child again, to a period when you were not so burdened down by time, when you were *Time-Light*. Now time weighs heavy because you have become time-heavy – rather, you have been submerged by the past and that which is dead and finished.

To fall back in love with your life, you must exorcise the ghosts of the past. The buzz of being is found only in the now, and the now knows nothing of the past or any future.

DAY 5 ▶ Stopping time

For Day 5, we are introducing a new exercise, so, again, write Day 5 in the top-left corner, draw up the sections you created for Day 4, but leave space for the new exercise, which you should title "Stopping time."

The narrative from the Past time-body stands in the way of the buzz of being. While your life is a constant becoming – a moving to something better – you are not being, you are becoming. Only a human being, not a human becoming, can fall back in love with his or her life. In the last few days, we have practiced some exercises to slow that movement of time; in today's exercise, we are going to endeavor to stop it altogether.

Do you recall the little experiment we tried on the very first day of the program when I wanted you really to look at something – a flower in your garden or someone's face? If you did try it, you may have noticed that the space between you and the object disappeared, and it seemed that time stopped, too.

That's because a life that is fully conscious doesn't live by an unconscious narrative from the past, but from the here and now, the vibrant present. The here and now is clearly the only actuality – it cannot be the half-remembered past or some projected future – and so the only way to live is fully to connect with the present. When you see, hear, taste, smell, read the newspaper, walk in the street, and engage in the countless other things you do every day, you must do so fully. We spend the day sleepwalking, or thinking – which, unless it's problem solving, is the past imprinting itself on the now. This imprinting is pervasive: whenever we see someone we have met before, we don't really see them at all but instead immediately impose a past image on them. When we look at a flower, it triggers a chain of thoughts about the fact that we need to do some weeding next weekend. When we see our office building, we think about the awful meeting we are due to have there today. And so it goes, all day, every day.

While the amount of imprinting we do almost every moment is extraordinary, the movement itself couldn't be simpler to observe; it's always from the past to the future, bypassing the present. That future could be just a few seconds ahead, but the imprinting can never be related to the current moment – because you are living that right now, even if you are not conscious that you are.

While thinking appears to happen in present time, it is, in fact, the movement from a half-experienced past to an imagined future: You cannot think about present time until it is past, even though it may be just a fraction of a second later. If you have a complete experience in the present, there is no thought at all. We have all experienced that: at the point of orgasm, for instance or during the scary moments of a roller-coaster ride.

During those moments, we are utterly at one with the present, and because it is so rich and complete, we want to have the experience again and again. We let go of the desire for a repeat or replay of an ecstatic moment only when we are conscious of the process. Until we are, we will continue to associate the extraordinary feeling with the experience itself, and so try to repeat it by replicating the circumstances. You may experience an overwhelming sense of joy and completeness when you are in a friend's sports car, for example. This creates an energy print in the Past time-body that wants that experience again, and because it was an association with a sports car, you will not rest until you purchase a sports car for yourself. Somehow, a sports car is associated with happiness and joy, even though the feeling actually occurred because you were present.

Only when we are fully conscious does the process of past-creating stop. When we are not creating from the thought store of the past, we do not project into a supposed future, and we are finally free to live fully in the present.

So far, we have been recording our thoughts and trying to understand from which center they come. Now we are going to extend the little experiment we started on the very first day to see if thought can come to a complete stop, just for a little while. There is no force or coercion involved, and I do not want you to try, in the sense of making a big effort. If you try to stop thinking, you will attempt to do so because you imagine that there is a bigger reward at the end of the process – and that merely creates yet another line of thought. To stop thinking, we are not going to try to stop the process. Instead, we are going to fall naturally and easily into life, by absorbing ourselves in it, as we did when we really looked at a flower, as though we were seeing it for the first time.

This time I want you to experience your hand, again as if you have never properly seen it before (which, by the way, you probably haven't). With our first exercise on Day 1, I asked you just to look at a flower – I didn't ask you to touch it or smell it. Today, I want you to experience with all your senses. I want you to look intently at your hand, observe the fine hairs on its surface, the blue veins, the knuckles, the nails and cuticles. I'd like you to touch your hand; what does that feel like? Smell your hand. Be aware of the energy pulsing through your hand, the tingling of the fingers, the duller sense of the palm. Now, close your eyes and really feel the hand with your senses fully alive. All of this will take only a minute or so – but in that short time, you didn't think. Thinking just stopped naturally. For that time you were fully conscious. There was no narrative to accompany the observing and sensing.

When there is no naming, no narrative, the true mystery of all things reveals itself as something beyond words. Everything in the world is remarkable because it is mysterious. You cannot know things in the way that your rational brain would like to comprehend; the thinking brain is in time and space, and the mystery of things sits beyond both dimensions.

You can freeze-frame time with any object or thing. A tree is a good target; approach it as though you had never seen a tree before. Don't try to classify it or even name it as a "tree." Don't bring up memories you may have about it – it could be the tree your son fell from, but let such thoughts go. Look at it from a distance so that you see it in its totality. Slowly walk toward it; now the very top may not be visible. Feel the trunk, the branches, and the leaves. Just absorb the miracle of its life, of life itself, a life that is beyond words and thoughts, which is how life is in its true form.

You can freeze-frame anything at any time. Try to do so at least once every day. If you are at work, study your desk or your clothes; when you are on the train, look at the other faces or the smears on the window. When you walk home, look at the sidewalk as though you had never seen it before. See it as new and different.

Look without words, without thoughts, without narrative. Not only will you truly see, possibly for the first time, but you will also be outside of psychological time. The movement of past to future will cease. The constant narrative of your life will fall silent. The Potential center, your third self, will shine through.

DAY 6 ▶ I am a camera

I am a camera with its shutter open, quite passive, recording, not thinking. Recording the man shaving at the window opposite and the woman in the kimono washing her hair.

Christopher Isherwood from *Goodbye to Berlin*, 1939

A new exercise for Day 6 – and by this stage you are likely to need an extra page, so each day henceforth will require three pages of note-taking. Begin by adding the new day in the top-left corner and then copying the sections you laid out for the previous few days. This time, however, we are adding a new section (for which the third page may be necessary), called "I am a camera."

The past is the filter through which you see the present, and its initial form of communication is an energy pulse, or uprush of feeling, which can be subtle or forceful. This pulse is almost instantaneously defined by the brain, with words and thoughts or feelings. This has the effect of strengthening the pulse; a pulse that is translated as "angry" will make you angrier still.

Anger also comes from the Present time-body, but this is in response to an immediate situation with which the body is faced, and it is a natural, even healthy, reaction. However, as with the uprush from the Past self, the anger from the Present self is also quickly defined, at which point the feeling ceases to be in the moment, and instead becomes part of the past.

This is a well-known phenomenon; it's often called "becoming self-conscious." The Present time-body reacts, and in that moment, your body is absolutely at one with the situation, but within seconds, a split occurs, and you almost see yourself being angry as if you were outside of the situation, observing yourself as a bystander would. At that point, the process of "anger-making" may stop – as it would if you were conscious of the process – or you may allow the brain's acknowledgement that you are angry to fuel the emotion and give it life beyond the moment, and beyond that which is necessary for the situation.

Sometimes, though, we become embarrassed by our behavior when the split occurs. A new emotion may come into play to deflect from the original display of feeling, or we may apologize, wondering what came over us.

The split – that rare moment between an honest feeling from the Present time-body and the subsequent reaction that seems to take over – is a perfect example of two of the time-bodies functioning almost as one. The emotion shifts from the Present to the Past time-body, where it is sustained by a defining of the initial feeling. Without words and definitions, the pulse, or uprush of feeling, loses its energy. Such is the importance of words, thoughts and feelings: they keep alive the past.

They are also vital, of course, as they are the *lingua franca* of the conceptual mind. We need them in order to make our way through the world, to create things and to make life more comfortable or easier. When the conceptual mind is problem solving, it is functioning healthily. However, the conceptual mind is like a child with attention deficit on sugar: It just does not know when to stop. It creates concepts about everything, as we have already seen. Your body is a concept, as is time and space, the "world" and your place in it, and indeed everyone you meet. It is almost impossible for you to see anything any more except through a concept, and, as a result, we do not really see anything at all. That is why, in an earlier exercise, I invited you to freeze-frame life, and really experience things that are in front of you.

Another important aspect of freeze-framing is to witness

without words. Words not only have the dual function of fueling concepts and of giving life to a pulse from the Past time-body, they also make possible the constant commentary and meaningless jabber that broadcasts to you every moment. So part of becoming conscious – of falling back in love with your life – is to live and experience without words and definition. Although words are a constant companion in your life, you would be astonished by how little you need them. For this exercise, I invite you to switch them off.

When the writer Christopher Isherwood coined the phrase "I am a camera," he meant that he was merely a lens, recording whatever was in front of him, without comment or judgment, and that's a good description of our next exercise. I want you to become a camera, sweeping around a room or office, just observing, but without words. When your eyes alight on a television set, don't record "television set"; instead, just observe it as a something in the room. The same goes for everything that enters your field of vision: a tree ceases to be "a tree," but is just a large shape with certain smells and features that you experience. As the Bible suggests, be like a stranger in a strange land. You don't know the name for anything you see, you don't know what is in front of you, other than the obvious fact that something is.

That way you will connect with the person or object in front of you. Instead of seeing it through a lazy label – a tree, a bird, a cloud – you see it for what it truly is, in all its magnificent mystery. A tree is not really "a tree" – which, after all, is merely a word or concept – it is a mysterious something, and the same goes for everything you witness every day.

To do this properly, you need to be quiet, and you need the time. It is not a great moment to try this when you are rushing to get the children to school or catch the train to the office. Instead, choose a moment when you have the time, when you are sitting down in the evening on the train or in the car.

As with all these exercises, the important thing is to practice a little every day. You can do this exercise in a minute or so. As you practice, you can extend the exercise until you are able to maintain it for an entire evening. You could watch television without using words or defining what you see. You could tune out the words being spoken by the actors so they become meaningless to you, just a wash of sounds, as if they were playing musical notes instead of speaking.

Once you have carried out this exercise a few times, you will see just how marvelous your brain truly is. It switches to words and concepts the moment they are required – to problem-solve or to deal with some issue that has arisen – before returning to camera mode, its natural resting state.

The more you consciously switch to camera, the more it will begin happening naturally by itself without any prompting. Before long, your brain will be retrained to work, as it should, responding as necessary instead of as the chattering monkey it is right now.

Without words, the space between "you" and the "world" will shrink and there will be no division between subject and object, you and the world – because you will cease to be the pivotal point of reference. A more accurate – and clumsier – expression of this state is seeing that there is no division.

So get your camera rolling.

DAY 7 ▶ Changing the tape

Another new exercise from Day 7 onward. You really will need that three-pages-per-day format now! Write "Day 7" in the top lefthand corner, copy the sections from Day 6, this time adding a new section on page three – "Changing the tape." And another thing – tie a piece of cotton around your wrist today.

Our thoughts create our world. They are based on unexamined assumptions about the world and ourselves, which are themselves created from partially observed experiences. These thoughts, feelings, and assumptions are given potency by the third body, the Potential, the field of all possibility.

Although we almost never become conscious of them, our thought narratives are a conjunction of beliefs. You might maintain that life is hard, money doesn't grow on trees, and you have to push if you're going to succeed in life. All these beliefs are interpretations of past events that were never fully understood – or were narratives started by parents, teachers or friends that we have absorbed. Something happened at a certain time or your parents told you something when you were at an influential age, and it started a narrative running.

Consequently, we walk around with these unspoken assumptions, busily discovering the world we have chosen to create. Money will always be hard to come by if that is what we've been told, and this becomes our truth for several reasons. At the prosaic level, it is because the thought forms ensure that there will always be difficulties about money and getting it, and this will further endorse an existing thought pattern. We will not recognize any evidence that disproves the belief, even when we encounter it, because our focus while we wear the "life is hard" spectacles will always be looking to confirm our initial belief. This is one of the hardest things to come to grips with: your life, for good or bad, has been your choice. You are responsible – to an extent that would startle you. You will find whatever it is that you are seeking, and you will live a life that is aligned with your thoughts. Although it has been an unconscious process, you have nonetheless decided to live according to a negative narrative. You are your own self-fulfilling prophet, usually of doom.

Now that you know this, you can change the tape. First, look for a pattern in your life. Money might be an issue, or you may have problems maintaining a long-term relationship with someone, or difficulty with time-keeping. Whatever the pattern – and there will be one or more – it is a good indicator of your own narrative.

Let us assume for a moment that money is always an issue in your life. This suggests that the narrative you have running maintains that money is a scarce resource. So today, we are going consciously to change the tape. At every available moment when you remember, I would like you to think: money is easy to come by; it is in ready supply; there is never a lack.

It will be easy to do this the first few times, but you will soon forget and fall back to sleep, hypnotized by your unconscious narrative. To help jog you awake, write down these thoughts in your log book and put an elastic band or a piece of cotton around your wrist. As you do so, tell yourself that it is there to act as a reminder to look in your notepad.

If the first day isn't too successful, don't worry – do it again the next day. As with maintaining attention on the present moment, the conscious narrative is a muscle that needs exercising, and it will get better the more you do it. As you do so, you will start seeing examples in your life that suggest money is easier to come by than you used to believe. Acknowledge this new fact, which will give you fresh energy to continue with the conscious narrative.

There is no end to the positive narrative tapes you can play for yourself. You can play one that tells you that you are a valuable and worthwhile person; another that tells you that you are talented and respected. And here is a Sunday special: Tell yourself that everyone is divine, and when you look into the eyes of another, you are looking at God.

It isn't that these positive narratives are necessarily any more "true" than the negative ones. The belief that money grows on trees is no more true than the belief that it doesn't. *It is what you determine to be true that matters*. This exercise has nothing to do with absolute truths. As we have already seen, there are no absolute truths in our world of time and space.

Truth or reality has everything to do with choice. You choose to continue running the negative narrative, albeit unconsciously, or you begin to wake up and consciously change the tape.

As the tape changes, so will your reality. It is important that you begin looking out for small changes in your life, because they will start occurring. Often, these signals of change were there before, but you just chose to ignore them because you had already told yourself that life cannot change.

When you witness these changes, be thankful for them and give yourself a little smile. After all, you have stumbled upon a most remarkable gift: that you are responsible. Although once this may have been the scariest thought imaginable, welcome it now because it is a power you can use.

Life will cease to be something that just happens to you and instead becomes something that you can begin to change and meld. Best of all, as you experiment with bringing change consciously into your life, you can have enormous fun. Remember, though, that conscious change is just a small part of waking up, and it is but one aspect of a much larger process starting to unfold.

Ironically, when you were unconscious, you may have wanted to be a Master of the Universe. Well, guess what? You are one.

DAY 8 ▶ Dealing with resentment

A new day, a new exercise. As always, start a new page, and write Day 8 in the top lefthand corner. Copy across all the previous exercises and sections, and add the new exercise "Dealing with resentment."

All of our exercises are about becoming aware of the movement from the Past time-body, and especially the Psychological past into the Present. Being aware is all you have to do. Any attempt or effort to change the pattern comes from the Past, which is constantly seeking resolution or a reward, such as enlightenment or never-ending joy.

Because of this movement, you are being short-changed. You are not living in the moment, but experiencing everything through a filter from the Past time-body: past feelings, past thoughts, past perceptions, past images.

We have seen that our feelings, thoughts, and perceptions filtered by the Past time-body begin with a pulse that is instantaneously translated into a thought or emotion. When you see someone whom you have met before, you have an immediate feeling about that person, based on your previous encounter with him or her. The true and honest response to any person or situation is a neutral one.

As everything is in a constant state of flux, the person and the situation are completely different from your previous encounter. Nevertheless, that is how it remains for you, as though the experience and the person were stuck in aspic.

Your feelings about that person may range from mild indifference to a strong dislike, even resentment. Although I have called today's exercise "Dealing with resentment," it concerns any emotion that is robbing you of the full experience in the present. As it is a new exercise, you will probably start catching yourself having a feeling about a person or a place only after the fact. This happens because you are not conscious enough to be able to catch the emotion in flight.

So, to begin, it is enough for you to reflect back on a feeling you had, whether it was a few moments ago or one that you had an hour or more ago. Either way, don't worry – just record it in your Work Book. Think of any occasion in the recent past when you felt some sense of resentment, hurt, anger, frustration, or irritation. Write down the occasion, the details and your feelings about it. As with all these exercises, don't judge or condemn.

As you continue with this exercise, the time between an event and your realization of a certain feeling about it will shorten. You may start out becoming conscious of the feeling a full hour afterwards, but the more you do this, the shorter the time gap will become, until you become conscious in that moment. At that point, feelings and thoughts about any situation in front of you will stop naturally.

DAY 9 ▶ Forgiveness + gratitude

A new day, a new exercise or two. Create a new three or four-page diary for Day 9, copy across the sections from Day 8, and add a new section on the third page: "Forgiveness + gratitude".

Our work on becoming conscious is getting interesting. Your log should be filling up with some of the thoughts you have monitored and their origins, whether from the Present, Past, or Potential centers. You have also had a go at stopping psychological time by experiencing with all your senses. You have looked dispassionately at something you held as true about someone. You have become a camera. And you have ejected your unconscious tapes, and instead installed and played some positive tapes of your own.

Today, I am adding another two tasks to the workload. Every day henceforth, I want you to be grateful for something in your life, and I also want you to forgive someone.

Being grateful for something is not so hard – or shouldn't be. The daily grind overwhelms us, and it is too easy to overlook the thousands of things for which we should be grateful every day. You can be grateful for your feet taking you to the train or the sidewalk for making your going easier. You could be thankful for the car that slowed to let you cross the street or for your heart, which keeps beating. You could celebrate your lungs for breathing in and out, and for the air that lets you live. How about the food you are given every day, and your children, your husband or wife? Whatever you choose, make it the subject of your conscious gratitude for the day. Write it down and date it in your log, and refer to it throughout the day.

But here's the thing – I want you really to mean it. This is not a form-filling exercise – your feelings should flow from the heart, and you should express your gratitude with passion. Feel your gratitude when you express it, ideally aloud. If that is difficult, and you aren't alone when you are carrying out the exercise, at least say it with meaning to yourself. And when you say it to yourself, do so with a little smile on your lips as you think of that person or thing for which you are grateful.

The other daily exercise is to forgive someone or some situation. This may be a tougher exercise than your gratitude diary because, as we saw in an earlier exercise, true forgiveness comes naturally only from complete understanding. However, if you are carrying out the exercises diligently, you are starting to wake up. It is worth pushing yourself to see if you can swim in the warm waters of forgiveness.

Our pride usually gets in the way of forgiving. We do not truly believe another person deserves to be forgiven; after all, he or she was awful to you. You suffered as a result – so why forgive? Here's why: By not forgiving, you have built more psychological time, and that stands between you and falling back in love with your life. Being resentful isn't hurting anybody but you. The person who harmed you isn't feeling that sense of resentment, is he? But you are. So not only did you suffer in the first place, you are continuing to suffer now and every day.

Although we are not conscious that we are still resenting someone or some past situation, that state of mind is the currency of the Past time-body; it is unconscious. Hardly a day goes by when somebody doesn't give us cause to get angry or irritated, especially when we are unconscious. It could be from a careless motorist who drives in front of us, forcing us to stop, a work colleague who doesn't do something he promised, or your partner or spouse who says something that upset you. It might even be the man in the coffee shop, who forgot to put mayo on your sandwich.

One way of testing if there remains a trace of a past upset is to imagine the person or situation involved and sense if any pulse of energy, or slight uprising of feeling, occurs as a result. If it does, you still have an unconscious memory of the experience. You need to let it go – otherwise, this ghost of an experience will continue to haunt your present, and you will not have a full connection to the here and now.

As you start the exercise, it is better if you begin with a relatively insignificant upset – such as the man in the cafe who forgot the mayo. Whatever it is, write down the words of forgiveness in your log, such as: "To the sandwich man, I truly and deeply forgive you from the bottom of my heart for forgetting the mayo today. I am releasing you, and I will not carry the burden with me. You are dissolved in my love." You can choose your own words, so long as you get across that meaning.

One important part of forgiving is adopting a wider perspective in order to understand why the event happened. In the case of the forgotten mayo, the sandwich man was busy, and he forgot. You can take the same perspective with the person who cut you off when you were driving. He may have been late for collecting his child from school and so was in a rush, and consequently misjudged the distance and your speed. These inconsequential events in your daily life offer a great opportunity for you to practice your forgiveness skills.

Once you have tried this a few times, you will see more and more opportunities where you can practice forgiveness. Interestingly, forgiveness is a movement of the Potential center, and the more you wake up, the more the Potential will become part of your life. Waking up is a process of being present in the here and now, and, for that to happen, the past must loosen its hold. But that can happen only when you become conscious of the Past time-body.

A partially observed experience becomes trapped in the Past time-body, where it continues to have a half-life, trying to complete itself. It wants resolution, and that is why the past continues to live in you. The practice of forgiveness brings the old hurt back into your life, as if it were still happening, and completes it. Once completed, the energy dissipates and vanishes. Your burden is lighter, and the here and now becomes more vivid.

Forgiveness and gratitude are processes for bringing you into the present, and allowing you to start falling back in love with your life.

Day ▶ 10 Kindness to the animal, part I

Although it is an exercise, Day 10 introduces a series of recommendations for keeping the body healthy. By this point, you'll need four pages per day. So copy everything across from Day 9, giving everything a little more space this time, and then add a new section: "Kindness to the Animal." You may already be carrying out many of the things recommended in this exercise – but write down anything new that you can introduce to make your body healthier. By the way, are you still wearing that piece of string?

It is time to move our focus from the Past time-body, where all our efforts have been concentrated so far, and to give a little loving kindness to the Present. The Buddha realized early in his quest that nothing could be achieved by a body that was starved of food, sleep, and water. It is important that you also understand this and give the body what it needs, without the deafening clamor of the Past time-body and its calls for comfort, which will lead you astray.

The needs of the Present time-body are quite simple, and yet it is extraordinary how people get it so wrong. Just look at the numbers of overweight and obese people, the thousands who die from an avoidable cancer every day, the millions who suppress their illness with a powerful drug.

The Present time-body just needs pure water, organic food, plenty of rest, reasonable amounts of exercise, and air that is good to breathe. Its brain and conceptual mind need to have problems to solve in order to keep sharp.

This simple approach is sabotaged by the needs of the Past time-body, which always believes it deserves rewards – of processed foods, cigarettes, alcohol and drugs – and which keeps playing the endless tape loops through the mind that eventually create anxiety, depression, and worse.

As you become more conscious – as the Potential center becomes more apparent – many bad habits will naturally fall away by themselves. You can help the process by introducing habits that are healthy for the Present time-body. You have probably incorporated some, if not many, of these into your diet and lifestyle already, but here's a quick checklist of the important ones to begin exploring from day 10 onwards. It's possible to write only briefly about each of these topics.

Understand your metabolic type: Many wonder if they should become a vegetarian and ethically they should. All animals have access to the Potential center, which is why they display great intelligence, empathy, and compassion. A failure to understand this is one of the great oversights of classic evolutionary theory. Although that is the absolute truth, your body may not yet be ready to embrace a vegetarian diet. One way to find out is to discover your own metabolic type, as some people need to eat meat until their Potential center has become more apparent. Metabolic typing uncovers the diet that is right for your body now, and some cancer sufferers have even seen their cancer disappear just by adapting to a diet that is appropriate for their body. To discover the type you are, go to the website: www.healthexcel.com for an initial review.

Maintain a correct acid/alkaline balance: Many chronic diseases are due to an acid/alkaline imbalance, and conventional wisdom has it that a high protein diet of meats, eggs, nuts, and some grains creates acid, while fruits and vegetables are alkali forming. Although this is the reason that so many suffer from a wide range of chronic diseases with the West's high-protein diet, the process is complicated by metabolic type. Foods can either acidify or alkalinize, depending on your specific type.

Don't eliminate fats from your diet: We live in a low-fat-foods society. This is entirely based on the belief that high cholesterol is bad for us, and is the cause of chronic heart disease. However, several studies suggest that cholesterol would have to be at a far higher level than what is now considered the current "danger" mark before it starts causing damage to the heart and arteries. Furthermore, fats are necessary; they play an essential role in maintaining a healthy body, and are one of the most vital ingredients for a functioning brain. This is why cholesterol-lowering statin drugs are often associated with memory loss and general mental decline; they reduce cholesterol to dangerously low levels. Cholesterol is even more important as we age, when we need fats and cholesterol in order to "feed" our brain.

Avoid processed foods: As a simple rule of thumb, do not eat anything that doesn't come directly from nature. Avoid anything that is white when it should be brown, frozen when it should be fresh, or laden with preservatives, flavorings, artificial sweeteners and other "helpful" added chemicals, rather than natural. In short, if it has been in a processing plant, don't buy it and certainly don't eat it.

Eat and drink organic: Whenever possible, try to eat and drink organic foods and drinks. Organic food is more expensive and its shelf life shorter because it hasn't been shot full of pesticides and preservatives, but at least you know you are getting more nutrition for your money.

Drink filtered water: You need to drink plenty of liquid every day. It's debatable just how much, but listen carefully to your body, which will tell you when and how much you need to drink. Use a good filter to ensure that all chemicals, heavy metals, parasites and fluoride have been removed first – or buy mineral water, preferably supplied in glass bottles, as toxins leach from plastic ones.

Be careful with pharmaceuticals: Prescription drugs can be important in the early stages of any disease, as they help suppress the worst symptoms, such as pain and discomfort. However, they are a short-term remedy, and you should always be looking for the underlying cause of any disease. Drugs cure nothing; they merely help make life bearable. Nevertheless, you run the very real risk of a chemical chain reaction that causes a whole host of side effects.

Get the omega-3/6 balance right: The omega 3 and 6 balance is just as important as the acid/alkaline one. The standard Western diet causes an imbalance of these essential fatty acids. The average person's ratio is 1 to 20 in favour of omega 6, when the ideal is 1 to 1. Again, this is a reflection of the amount of processed foods we eat, as vegetable oils, salad dressings, and margarines are rich in omega 6. Omega 3-rich foods include linseed, cod liver oil, and fresh, cold-water oily fish such as salmon, tuna, mackerel, and herring.

Get adequate vitamin D: Scientists have only recently begun to understand the vital importance that vitamin D plays in our general health, especially our mental health. The most plentiful source is, of course, sunshine, but we have been so warned off by skin cancer scares that most of us are starved of this nutrient. It is important to get an hour's sunshine every day. Top up your vitamin D levels with nutritional supplements or foods such as milk, eggs, yoghurt, and fatty fish.

Keep your home chemical free: It is hard to escape all the chemicals in household products and toiletries, but you can eliminate some of them by buying "green" and chemical-free cleaners, air fresheners, shampoos, and make-up. Even the paint on our walls and the carpets under our feet are leaching chemicals all the time. Keep your chemical load to reasonable levels. A healthy immune system can handle a level of toxins, but it shouldn't become overwhelmed.

Get seven hours of sleep: A good night's sleep is essential. Without it, some of the other exercises in this program will seem overly difficult. It is the natural end of a day that has been well spent, with activity and proper and nutritious food. For some, sleep is elusive; if you fall into that unhappy category, here are a few things to introduce into your daily regime. Eat lightly in the evening, and don't eat too late. Ensure your last shot of caffeine is taken no later than 2pm. Don't watch TV just before you go to bed; stop watching television an hour beforehand, and instead pick up a book to read, ideally one that is either philosophical or spiritual. Listen to some calming music, such as a quiet piece of classical music or ambient, which has a hypnotic effect. Try to quiet the mind through meditation, although researchers have found this is most effective when you do so midway through the day, and not immediately before you go to bed. Another sleep aid is blackout curtains, which make the room completely dark.

Have a good breakfast: It is a truism that the most important meal of the day is breakfast. The best breakfast should include oatmeal, one of the healthiest starts to any day, and it's healthier still when it is topped with pure maple syrup and berries.

Exercise every day: You don't have to sweat it out at the gym, but the body does need to exercise every day. A good vigorous walk is sufficient – and that means around 100 steps per minute, for 20 minutes. That's enough to get everything exercised, and to get the heart beating a little faster. When you're on the walk, breathe in deeply and fill the lungs. If a walk is difficult because of problems such as arthritis, try swimming every day.

Don't immediately kill a fever: Medicine views a fever as a major alert and it swings into action immediately to bring it down as quickly as possible. Although an unusually high fever can be dangerous, it is a necessary process. It helps kickstart the immune system, kills off germs and viruses, and even eliminates diseases such as cancer in their early stages. If you do develop a fever, monitor it very carefully and allow it to run for several days before seeking to bring down your temperature. Make sure you drink plenty of liquids and rest in a room that is properly aired.

Breathe properly: It is an extraordinary fact that most of us don't breathe properly. We often have very shallow breaths, and some of us breathe through our mouth. We should take frequent deep breaths through our nose, filling our lungs so that they swell with health-giving oxygen, and then release the air slowly through our mouth.

Keep your gums healthy: Doctors are only now beginning to understand the importance of gums and teeth to our overall health.

Many health problems, especially heart disease, are associated with poor gums and teeth. Inflamed gums that frequently bleed are very likely causing problems throughout the body. In addition, it is important to keep amalgam fillings down to a minimum and avoid root canal work wherever possible. Health researcher and pioneering dentist Weston Price discovered a direct correlation between the health of specific teeth and the health of organs in the body. He believed that root-canal work caused bacterial leakage, which is responsible for systemic autoimmune diseases such as arthritis. You are also most likely to encounter an X-ray in the dentist's chair, and so restrict these to only essential work.

Avoid smoking and drink in moderation: It goes without saying: if you are a smoker, stop today. Self-hypnosis programs can help wean you off the weed. With alcohol, moderation is the key. A glass of wine every so often may do more good than harm, but it is important to have quite a few alcohol-free days every week in order to allow the body restore itself.

This advice has but one result in mind: to maintain the body's health so that it doesn't stand in the way of carrying out the *Time-Light* program. Pain, a lack of sleep, bodily discomfort – all of these loom large and overshadow all else. A healthy body is invisible; just listen to its needs, and its own intelligence will guide you.

Day 11: Kindness to the animal, part II

*Not so much a new exercise today as helpful advice about
mental health and well-being (which comes from the proper
functioning of the brain). So, for Day 11, create a new four-
page spread, using all the sections you used for Day 10. If you
do not suffer from chronic and clinical depression, this
exercise may not be relevant to you, although it's still worth
reading.*

If you suffer from chronic depression – particularly if you are
taking prescription medication – you need to go beyond the
commonsense dietary advice offered in the previous chapter and
become a medical detective. It is vital that you don't go it alone;
work closely with a qualified health professional. No matter from
what discipline, he or she must be sympathetic to the idea that
chronic depression has a biochemical aspect.

Although transient and mild depression is something we all
suffer from time to time, chronic depression is a problem that
persists. Antidepressants and other drugs such as the
antipsychotics may have their place in treating serious
depression, but they do not address the underlying problem. As
they are very powerful chemical agents, they come with equally
powerful side effects.

Almost certainly, something in your life – in your immediate
environment or your diet – is causing your depression. It
could be a chronic food allergy – and always suspect dairy or
gluten first – or even leaks from a gas cooker could be
responsible. Although all the exercises in the *Time-Light*
program are likely to be helpful in alleviating symptoms, they
will not overcome a biochemical reaction. In that case, the
cause has to be eliminated, and it may take several months of

detox before you are feeling well again.

If you suspect that foods may be responsible for your depression, the first foods to eliminate are wheat and dairy, which together are responsible for the majority of food allergies and intolerances. If you feel depressed or down after eating a sandwich or some other wheat-based food, it's one clue that wheat could be the problem. Today there are plenty of wheat- and gluten-free alternatives, and so you don't need to go without your daily bread. The same goes for dairy products; many milk, cheese and butter alternatives are available on the market.

The cause is just as likely to be from a chemical or toxin in your immediate environment: your gas stove, your central heating system, the toiletries you use, the air freshener, or something else in your home. Environmental toxins have a cumulative effect; the body's immune system has been likened to a water barrel that starts to overflow when too much rainwater is added. Just removing a few toxins from your environment might be enough to bring down your body's overall load, allowing your immune system to begin expelling poisons in your body.

Hypothyroidism, or underactive thyroid, is another unsuspected cause of chronic depression. Although most of us are familiar with its opposite, hyperthyroidism – when the thyroid gland is overactive – many of us suffer from an underactive gland, a problem that can be brought on by diet and stress. Once diagnosed, it is relatively easy to resolve, but don't self-medicate. Instead, seek out a sympathetic health practitioner.

The *Time-Light* program is not designed as a self-help course for overcoming major stress or trauma. Several modalities, such as Emotional Freedom Technique and Thought Field Therapy, have been successful in treating chronic depression and anxiety, and you may wish to explore these as a complement to this program.

Day 12 ▶ Changing personality patterns

A new exercise today. Create a four- or five-page spread for Day 12 and add a new section: "Changing personality patterns."

Ever since we were children, somebody has been telling us to do things differently. We were told to sit up straight and not to slouch, to chew our food properly, not to talk with our mouths full, to wash behind our ears, to go to bed on time. We were also told we had to become a better person. We should be more patient, we should respect others, and we should be kind to the elderly and to animals. We should always be polite.

The edicts about washing and eating properly relate to the Present time-body, and these all can be achieved, provided we remember to follow them. It is possible to sit up straight or chew our food properly, if we have half a mind to do so, and we can wash behind our ears, if it's not too much bother.

But we cannot so easily follow the instructions to become a more patient person, respect others and be kind to the elderly, because our ability to do these depends on the extent of the power of the Past time-body, and that, as we now know, is unconscious – or, more precisely, its movements or energy pulses are not acknowledged.

The Past time-body governs most of the social niceties – such as being patient, kind and respecting others – that make the world a tolerable place. Because the Past time-body continually repeats the same pulses whenever the opportunity in present time allows, so these pulses are expressed as behavior patterns, which, in turn, create a "personality." How many times have you heard yourself say about someone, "Oh, he's always losing his temper," or "He's always impatient"? Patience and temper are aspects of unconscious behavior, the automatic defining of pulses from the Past time-body. While someone is unconscious or unaware of the Past time-body, he or she cannot change any personality tic.

When you look more closely at these personality traits, you see that they are a movement of psychological time from the past to the present. If you are impatient, it is because you believe you know what the future holds, one of the tricks of psychological time. Of course, you could be suddenly overcome with impatience because a delay means you may miss a train or an appointment, but often a person is impatient because of some perceived endpoint that is little more than a mental chimera. For people in the grip of this particular mental tape, the future always holds better things than does the present moment.

Whether you are walking the dog in the park, eating a meal with friends, or watching a film, your mind will eventually wish that you were somewhere else. The Czech writer Milan Kundera called one of his books *Life is Elsewhere* – and that perfectly describes how it is for impatient people. Life is always somewhere else and at some future time. Why? Because the Past time-body is the movement of psychological time, and the impetus that makes us work harder for a better job or a higher degree is the same one that projects a better future place and time – toward which the unconscious person is always drawn. In reality, someone in its thrall is merely postponing his or her life for an imagined and unattainable better life.

You can witness a similar movement in people who are anxious or stressed. There are many causes of stress, but one major catalyst is the imagined future. You imagine what will happen in the exam room, in the dentist's chair, during the meeting with the boss. Because of this movement of psychological time, you become stressed and anxious. We have all experienced this some time or another – and you probably discovered that each time you were wrong. It was not as bad as you feared or at least not how you imagined it would be.

Fear is one of the big building blocks of personality. In the Present time-body, it is a natural, even healthy response. You are right to be frightened if a mad bull is rushing towards you; that fear is translated into a chemical reaction that gives you extra speed or agility when it is most needed. However, once you are over the fence and safe, the fear from the Present time-body subsides and dissipates.

It is not the same for the Past time-body. At that level, the experience becomes a "trapped" emotion, which will be played out repeatedly, not necessarily as a fear of raging bulls, but as some undefined fear of something in the world. This adds to the person's general sense that the world is hostile.

As we have already seen, fear generated by the Past time-body is a playing out of psychological time. You fear a future, even though you cannot know what it holds; you fear a new experience or situation, even though you have no idea what will happen; you fear the next day, because you have some sense that the world is not a friendly place. As you see, all of these are movements through time – from a barely understood past to an imagined future, bypassing the present.

As with all our thought forms, fears cannot survive in the bright light of the conscious person. They need the demilight of the Past time-body so that they can spread their shadows over us. However, as with all shadows, they vanish in an instant when the light is switched on.

So, from day 12, we're going to switch on the light. You may already have a feeling for your own personality patterning: you may sense that you are impatient or are easily angered. If you're not sure, just ask someone close to you – they would love to tell you!

As with all these exercises, there's no right or wrong. It is not "wrong" that you get angry easily or that you are impatient, any more than it is wrong that a fly lands on your window. I just want you to observe the fascinating movement of psychological time. While you are attentive, nothing will happen, of course. Nevertheless, before long you will fall back into unconscious routines and your old pattern of impatience will reemerge. When it does, write it down in your log book. Simply record the fact that you were impatient and then analyze why. What were you doing at the time and what were you thinking about? Were you thinking that you could be doing something better? If so, why did you have that thought? Notice the movement of time and record that, too.

You may completely miss the first few instances, but try to catch yourself whenever you can, and slowly you will become more conscious of it. As we said at the beginning of the program, this is the most difficult thing in the world to do, so do not be hard on yourself should you fall back asleep. You have a lifetime of habitual thinking to overcome.

By practicing this exercise every day, the old pattern will disappear. After a while, people will start noticing. "You don't seem to be as impatient as you used to be," they will say, or "You used to get really angry about things like that – but look at you now."

Even your parents would be proud of you.

Day 13 Seeing the world as facts

A new exercise today – but note, it's without an arrow. This means that I want you to do this exercise on Day 13 only – don't do it again on Day 14 or any days afterward. So, in your four/five-page-per-day log, copy the sections across from Day 12, and then, on a new page, create a new section for today's one-day exercise: "Seeing the world as Facts."

All of us have something in our life that just doesn't work. It may have to do with money, with a relationship, with our career.

For today's exercise, I want you to see that the world is made up of facts. You are in debt. The washing machine doesn't work. Your boss won't give you a pay rise. The "world," that thing out there, is made up of nothing but facts like these. And you can't do much with a fact: you can choose to acknowledge it or not, you can act on it or not.

However, because we are unconscious beings, we do far more with facts than simply choosing to be active or passive about them. We get stressed over them, we have anxiety attacks, we cannot sleep because of them, we endlessly think about them, and we fret about them. At this point, the fact ceases to be a fact, and instead becomes something over which we become desperate, feel despondent, depressed, or helpless.

In sober moments, you know that worrying about a fact does not alter it. Indeed, it could make it worse because you are not even thinking logically any longer – and your worries could cause a pattern that attracts more of the same. However, come the wee small hours, come the time when you fall fully into the Past time-body, the same monkey mind starts churning again, and the fact takes on greater significance and becomes something over which you stress.

So, on Day 13 I want you to use your Work Book to write down all the problems you have now (that's why you have set aside a full page for this exercise). It might be that you are in debt, you are without a partner, your dog has died, or you have a dental appointment you are dreading. Whatever it may be, write it down. Then, beneath that, write down another problem in your life, and so on, down the page.

Now, next to each item, I want you to create two columns. At the top of one write: Actions. At the top of the second write: Inactions. Go down the list, one by one, and consider very carefully what actions you can take. If there is genuinely absolutely nothing you can do, tick that instead.

So, if you have a dreaded dental appointment, what can you do about it? You could cancel it, but that is a judgment only you can make based on any pain you are in or how urgently you need the work done. If you accept that it is necessary dental work, you have to tick the "Inaction" column. There's nothing you can do about it other than keep the appointment. There is nothing about the situation that you can change.

There are always times when we can do nothing. Sometimes it is not within our power to change the fact in any way. This is something that we must recognize and accept. When somebody we know dies, for example, there is nothing we can do about it. No amount of fretting or sleepless nights will change the fact. Although it is natural to grieve, we must not become dominated by our grief to such an extent that we are paralyzed by it.

Let's look at another problem. Suppose that you are in debt. Have you spoken to the person or organization to which you owe the money? If not, you can put in the "Action" column your intention to speak with them. Be specific. Note when you intend to speak to them and date the action. Could you borrow money from a relative to pay off the debt? Have you asked? Would you? If so, that is another item for the "Action" column. Again, choose a date when you plan to get in touch. Could you get more money from work? Have you asked the boss for a raise? How about putting yourself forward for promotion or for extra work? Have you put yourself in the boss's shoes? Can you think of things in your organization that don't work well, that could be more efficient? If you clearly see a way of improving that situation, why don't you present the problem – and your solution – to your boss? He might be so astonished that he may well give you that raise without your even having to ask for it. These are all things you could list in your Action column and plan to do in order to address the fact that you are in debt.

When you think through your options, it is important that you plan to act on anything that comes to mind. Set yourself a definite date when you will do it and then somehow pluck up the courage to act. If you don't, your Past time-body is again preventing you from acting by projecting into an imagined future. Until you pick up the telephone, you don't know what the response will be, so stop living in psychological time and just do it.

The same goes for your boss. You might see him as a difficult and unapproachable person, but it could be that he is looking for enterprising employees to take greater responsibility for helping to solve his business problems. Do not let the Past time-body hinder you. Be present and find out.

Once you complete this exercise, it is important to grasp that there really is nothing more you can do about being in debt, going to the dentist, or whatever situation you have chosen to examine. You have dealt with the facts that make up your world.

What you must not now do is create an internal world of the facts, as fueled by the Past time-body. After completing the exercise, be still, be clear and say – ideally aloud – that you should now stop worrying, that everything that can be done has been done.

As with all these exercises, you will almost certainly fall back into the patterns of the Past, and the old tapes will start their old refrain. Now you can catch yourself. When you do, remind yourself there is nothing to think or worry about. You have done everything that is possible to do.

The exercise brings its own stillness. The Past time-body will stop the automatic and unconscious fretting of its own accord. It will cease its striving for something better "out there" and at some time in the future. It will see the fact for what it is and, in that recognition, become still.

Day 14 Finding The Recorder

There's a new exercise today, so create a new five-page section, and copy across the areas from Day 12. Add a new section from today: "Finding The Recorder." Choose someone to share your feelings with and approach them about your intention to confide with them. If you're unable to find a Recorder today, put this exercise in the log for tomorrow. If for any reason it is impossible to find someone suitable, use a recording device of some sort instead.

So far, we have been having a private conversation with ourselves. We have been observing and writing down, analyzing and recording – but now we want to make the experience more real. As we enter the third week, it is time to share our thoughts and our observations with someone else.

For years you have been hypnotized by your internal monologue – the whole "reality-making" discourse from the Past time-body, defined and verbalized by the brain and its concepts. Its potency has come from the fact that its movement has taken place in darkness, in a shadow land of the Past. However, over the past two weeks, you have been exposing this movement to the light. You have been quietly observing the pulses and flickers from the Past time-body, and you have been recording them without judgment. You have a diary of your internal monologue, and while it is now something that has become conscious, it is still a silent one.

When we experience pulses that are defined by the conceptual brain, we see the world through a filter. We may express ourselves through that filter – we might say we do not like someone, or some situation, for example – and we are rarely challenged to explain why we think the way we do. In truth, we usually cannot explain the feeling we have or understand where it comes from.

As we now know, it comes from one or more of three places: the Present time-body has feelings, usually about a situation or a person, which suggest impending danger or threat. Feelings from the Present are invariably about new situations or with people we have not met before. The Potential center, too, sends out a pulse, and this we usually call intuition. We intuitively know that something is going to happen, as though the feeling has come from somewhere beyond space and time – which, of course, it has.

However, most of our feelings arise from the Past time-body, and these form the filter through which we interpret the world from moment to moment. These feelings from the Past time-body feed off the unconscious movement to the Present time-body, and they are empowered by our silence or tacit acceptance – and so now we want to talk about them. For this, you need The Recorder, somebody who will listen dispassionately, without judgment or even comment, to all the feelings you have observed and recorded. The Recorder can either be someone whom you absolutely trust or – oddly enough – a complete stranger.

The most likely Recorder is somebody close to you, such as your husband or wife, sister or brother, but this can present problems, because often when we are close to people, we have things that remain secret or private, which we would rather they did not know. If that is not a problem with you, go ahead and adopt him or her as your Recorder.

However, the ideal Recorder for you is more likely to be a complete stranger because it is easier to talk about your feelings and thoughts with someone you do not know, and in whom you do not have an emotional investment. But how can you approach such a person without their calling the police? One way is by logging on to the website that accompanies this book: www.time-light.com, where you can view a network of Recorders. The best way is to meet face-to-face as writing them an email isn't much better than the writing you've been doing in your diary already.

If there isn't a Recorder near where you live and you're uncomfortable about talking to someone close to you, the next best thing is to record your thoughts into a voice recorder. At least you are still vocalizing your thoughts and feelings from your diary observations.

If your Recorder is a person, his or her role could not be easier: They have to do nothing, absolutely nothing at all. They mustn't comment, make helpful remarks, smile, or try in any way to empathize or sympathize, raise an eyebrow, look shocked, laugh out loud, burst into tears or put an arm around you.

The Recorder is not there as a therapist or counselor. He or she is nothing more or less than a dispassionate pair of ears. It is the very act of verbalizing your thoughts and feelings as you have recorded them in your diary that offers the potency for change. It is like sitting in a shadowy room and imagining it full of ghosts. However, pull the curtains back, and the room is flooded with sunlight; the shadowy ghosts evaporate.

As you talk, the curtains are pulled back. The feelings lose their power, and they are finally seen for what they are.

Day 15 Right Thinking, Right Action, Right Feelings

Write Day 15 on the top lefthand corner of a new page, bring across the sections from Day 12 – include The Recorder again if you haven't yet completed this task – and add a new section for today, "Right Thinking, Right Action, Right Feelings." Note that this is not an ongoing exercise, but instead is just for today.

Today's exercise is one of taking stock. It comes right out of Buddhism – the exercises are a variation on the Eightfold Path of right view, right intention, right speech, right action, right livelihood, right effort, right mindfulness, and right concentration – although similar practices are also found in Christianity.

But what is "right"? For the Buddha, it is about steering a middle path through life, without overly engaging in it but also not withdrawing from it. This means that the actual terrain changes for each of the paths and can be open to interpretation.

But suppose we contemplate right thinking, action, and feelings from the viewpoint of the Three Selves. What is right thinking, right actions and right feelings in that case?

Right thinking: None of the Three Selves actually "thinks"; as energy centers, they send out pulses that are almost immediately translated into a thought by the brain in the Present time-body. It is important to understand how this process works and what thinking actually is before we attempt to define right thinking. Thoughts have enormous potency as they create an increase in the frequency of the pulses, which, in turn, triggers a vicious circle of thoughts and emotions. Right thinking, therefore, is composed of thoughts that are appropriate to the situation and of value. Most thinking is irrelevant and useless – indeed, most thinking is nothing more than the pointless commentary that accompanies almost every experience — and so most thinking is not right thinking at all.

For the Present time-body, right thinking is primarily problem solving. How do I fix this? How does that work? Thoughts that arise as pulses from the Past time-body are invariably a reiteration of an old experience, which is being chewed over repeatedly, in a vain and hopeless attempt to reach resolution. All of this is, by definition, wrong thinking. The only right thinking from the Past time-body is that which enables the viewing of a problem in context, without fanning the flames of anger. Right thinking from the Past time-body would be an attempt to understand, forgive and provide balm to a situation. So, in practical terms, it involves seeing the other's point of view – understanding, say, why somebody did something that has upset you. With the Potential center, we are creators and part of a unified field. Right thinking from this center includes such thoughts as that we are not alone, that, as cocreators, we are responsible for our life, and that we are compassionate to others who are suffering because they do not yet see the unified field of which they are a part.

Right action: All action is apparent in the Present time-body, even if it does not always start from there. Action that originates in the Present deals with immediate concerns of sufficiency, such as whether you have enough food, proper shelter and sexual satisfaction. Similar actions, originating in the Past time-body, concern having more than we need – a drive for more: more extravagant food, a bigger home, and either sex with multiple partners or pornography. Actions from the Potential center are expressions of a sense of unity, understanding, and forgiveness. As the latter is the natural state to which all life aspires, all right action, from any of the centers, is an expression of forgiveness.

Right feelings: For the Buddha, feelings involved attraction or repulsion, or were neutral. For us, feelings, or emotions, vary according to the time-bodies; for the Present, feelings concern immediate situations, giving rise to anger, fear, or surprise. The feelings should subside and disappear once the cause has gone away. For the Past, feelings are far more complicated and arise as part of a process that repeats an old experience. Most of us often get angry all over again about some supposed hurt that you suffered in the past. For the Potential self, feelings arise from love: a realization of the unity of all things – and from understanding.

So, for day 15, your exercise is to reflect on right thinking, action and feelings, and to observe the process. All thinking, action and feelings will become right naturally by themselves and without any effort or conscious observation of any code or precept as you follow the 21-day program. That is true religion.

Day 16 ▶ Responding, not reacting

A new exercise today, so write Day 16 in the top lefthand corner of a new page and copy across the grid from day 12. Then add a new category – "Responding, not reacting" – that will be part of the ongoing grid until day 21.

Most of us react to things in the world while we remain unconscious to the movement of time from the Past time-body. As you now know, a reaction is a blind, automatic act – often resulting from a sudden rising up of emotion. Sometimes we are aware of it only after the fact. Our reactions are invariably out of proportion to the circumstance and often embarrassing to us, especially afterward when we "wake up."

Reactions happen because a situation in the present resembles something that happened in the past, about which you retain an emotional charge. In other words, the new situation is one with a familiar pattern and the power to revive some unfinished business from the past. And, of course, everything that makes up the Past time-body is unfinished business.

You undergo this process on a daily basis, quite unaware that, in a sense, the Present is being possessed by the Past time-body. You as your Present self are being used and lived through by the Past of dead but incomplete experience.

By comparison, a response is a considered and sober act that is reasonable and appropriate to the circumstance. If you are able to live in the Present, you *respond* to situations because each experience is new and different. As conscious beings in the Present, we do not have the past imprinting itself and reestablishing a familiar pattern.

Not reacting doesn't mean we shouldn't respond, as this story from the Hindu faith demonstrates. An Indian sage so impressed a lion with his talk of peace and non-violence that the lion decided to renounce killing. Soon, word got around, and all its old adversaries started picking a fight with the lion, which refused to retaliate. Eventually, the lion had enough and staggered back, bloody and bowed, to the sage.

"What happened to you?" asked the sage.

"I've just been following your teachings of non-violence. Now look what's happened to me," said the lion, pointing to his wounds.

"Yes, you're right not to kill," said the sage, "But I never said anything about not roaring."

We have to roar sometimes, but as a controlled act and not a blind, lashing out from a place of emotional hurt. So, from today, your exercise is to watch for moments of reaction. While you watch you will not react, but in time you will fall back asleep, and the Past time-body will again take control. However, as with all the other exercises in this program, the times that you blindly react will become fewer as you slowly wake up to the movements from the Past.

Day 17 ▶ Going out into the world

A new exercise today. Create a new five-page log for Day 17, copying across all the sections from Day 16, and add a new section "Going out into the world." As you will see, it has an arrow with it, so this exercise should be a feature in all the remaining days of the program.

A psychiatric unit had a major staff shortage and the existing employees were seriously overworked. The doctors could not see outpatients who were chronically depressed and even suicidal in any reasonable time. The nursing staff realized that they had to stay in touch with the patients, even if they could not see them as often they would like. They needed to know the patients were taking their drugs and were not becoming suicidal – so they sent patients a postcard. On each card was a simple message: the hospital staff was thinking of them. If they really needed help, the nurses would find time for them. If they did not hear from the patient, they sent him or her a different postcard, about a month after the previous one had been mailed.

By coincidence, around that time the psychiatric unit was one of several dozen chosen by a group of independent researchers for a study into the efficacy of certain powerful antidepressants. After interviewing a cross-section of patients from each of the psychiatric units, the researchers concluded that those from this one particular unit were faring far better than those from any other unit. But why? The drugs were the same. The therapy was the same – in fact, the unit that came out on top was meeting with its patients less frequently than the others were. The only real difference between this unit and the others was the postcards. And that, of course, was the one difference that mattered. That simple act of contact had made the patients feel wanted, that someone genuinely cared. In almost every case, the patient felt that he or she mattered.

Such is the power of community and belonging – and that is going to be at the heart of the next exercise in our program. Speaking out loud to The Recorder, or into your voice recorder, was the first step of going out into the world and presenting who you are to another. Now we are moving further out to a social group.

A relationship with a social group or a community is vital for our health and sanity as we seek to make conscious the internal monologue of the Past time-body. It will also give you a wonderful sense of belonging and help to dissipate any feeling you may have that the world is hostile and unfriendly. A sense of belonging also releases us from the private prison of the past's patterns – just as the psychiatric-unit patients discovered.

Many of us live our lives within the confines of a nuclear family. We rarely see our neighbors because our fences are too high, we do not talk to people in our community because we have security gates, and we do not go out at night because we are frightened. The world has become a reflection of our own disconnectedness.

At this point in the program, we are working on bringing down our internal walls and allowing the daylight in to our unconscious activities – and as we lose the divisions in ourselves, the divisions between the world and us will also go. With this exercise, we are going to give the process a helpful, conscious push.

The point of the exercise is to engender a feeling of belonging by joining any social group, formal or informal. It could be the local drama society, the chess club, the Parents-Teachers Association (PTA), the Rotary Club, the local jogging and athletics club, or ramblers club if you are in Britain – anything you feel comfortable being a part of. If you are still holding on to beliefs (and we need to keep working on that) and you define yourself as a Republican or Conservative, joining the local Democrat or Labor club might not work for you.

Better yet, join up with people in your area who are also reading this book. Come to the website – www.time-light.com – for people in your community who are like-minded.

Remember, the idea of this particular exercise is not to reinforce any sense of a world out there as separate from you, but instead to rid yourself of any hostile thoughts or beliefs you might still have that the world is in some way unfriendly or even intimidating. The exercise is also designed to help you realize that you are not "you" any more than they are "they": we are all together.

Day 18 ▶ Seeing your fears away

Copy across all the sections from yesterday, putting Day 18 in the top lefthand corner. You also need to add a new section: "Seeing your fears away." This new section requires two columns: Put "Fear" as the heading for one column and "Origin" above the second.

You are afraid. It is the most common emotion at the very center of many of your core beliefs, and it shapes most of our actions – usually as movements away from the fear. As we saw with mirror patterns, your desire for money may be, at heart, a drive away from the fear of poverty; your desire for success may be a response to the fear of being unacknowledged; your desire for enlightenment may be spurred on by your fear of unhappiness.

Although it is one of the foundational emotions, fear is hidden from most of us. We are usually unaware that we are frightened. But, of course, fear is the perfect expression of the movement of psychological time from the past to an imagined future. Something bad may have happened in the past, and we project that into an imagined future. Sometimes we fear a future without having experienced anything similar in the past; some of us may have a morbid fear of being poor without having had direct experience of it, but we imagine, from an amalgam of past observations, what it must be like.

When you are frightened of something that you imagine will happen to you at some future point, you are suggesting that you can see ahead with absolute clarity, and that you can determine precisely what will befall you. You may fear going to the dentist, for example, because you can "see" exactly what will happen to you when you get there. Of course, nobody really knows what the future holds, and it is very rarely anything that we imagined it would be, but no matter how many times our forecast of events do not match the reality, we still hold a fear of much of our future.

By now, you are getting a good idea of how the process works. Your Past time-body – and all your time-bodies or centers, in fact – send out pulses that are immediately defined by the brain, which, in turn, superimposes thoughts, words, and feelings on them. By that process, pulses from the Past time-body create psychological time through which you see and understand the world, including yourself. All of this is the movement of past, or dead, emotion into a quasi-living state, which happens because you are unaware of it.

The emotions themselves are half-experienced or partially understood events from the past, and like ghosts that continue to inhabit their former homes these feelings are relived through you in order to complete the experience. Yet it is a hopeless endeavor. While this movement is happening, you are being denied the full and rich experience of the moment, which can happen only in the full experiencing of the timeless present.

That is the genesis and lifecycle of every thought and every emotion, and once you have observed that for yourself, you will understand how every emotion, including the foundation ones such as fear, develops. Again, it is important not to try to stop being afraid; when people urge you "not to be afraid," it is a pointless request while you remain unconscious, because the emotion of fear is living through you and you are unaware of that movement. Instead, it is sufficient to observe and record – and, eventually, to talk about your secret internal world to The Recorder or into your voice recorder.

Although the basic actions of observing, recording and vocalizing are useful, we have to dig a little deeper if we are to understand fear. Very few thoughts reveal themselves as being fear-based, but instead hide their original impetus. As we saw earlier, most thoughts and emotions are a reaction to fear, a moving away from it. Now that you are well into your third week of the program, you may have developed the stillness and subtlety that helps to reveal the fear beneath the thought. Fortunately, there are only a few basic fears: a fear of loss, of failure, of being unloved or feeling worthless, or of powerlessness. Extraordinarily, we do not have a fear of death, as you may recall from the first chapter. The reason, as we have seen, is because only the Present time-body dies, and since that lives in present time and deals with its direct needs, it cannot have fears of its future demise.

Any one of those basic fears – of loss, failure, being unloved, worthlessness or powerlessness – is likely to be the root of many of your thoughts through psychological time, from the past to the imagined future. So, for this exercise, we need an extra column – one that identifies the originating fear of any current thoughts you have. At first, you may be guessing, but after you try it for a few days, you will get better at identifying exactly the fear behind the process. This process, in which you not only observe and record, but also analyze, I call dynamic observing, and we will be using it again in the next exercise.

Dynamic observing requires the asking of open questions, to which you do not necessarily get — or even expect — a response. For this particular exercise, it is sufficient to keep asking: What is the root fear of this thought? A reasonable follow-on question might then be: Do I feel it is from a fear of loss? Or of failure? The key word here is "feel." You cannot know, and your analytical brain cannot help you. However, you can *feel* the answer, and the more you use the technique, the more you increase your ability to do so.

All the other exercises in the program, especially those drawing on vocalizing and community, are also working toward eliminating fear. You bring your fears into the open; you finally see them for what they truly are: phantoms that try to inhabit your living being.

Day 19 ▶ Unthreading your story

Another day, another new exercise. Again, copy across all the sections from Day 18 into a new day and add a new section: "Unthreading your story." If you are finding it difficult to write everything into five pages, simply spread your sections across to a sixth page – but remember to put the correct day at the top of each page.

In the previous exercise we introduced a new tool – dynamic observing – and you shall need it again today as you unthread your story. Your story is your implicit narrative about who you are and why you do what you do. It is the scaffolding around the emotions that have pulsed out from your Past time-body and been given substance by the conceptual brain.

Your story is your narrative; it tells you everything about the world and yourself that you think you know. It is not true, of course, because you are imposing concepts onto a dynamic, changing present. It derives from a half-seen experience that seeks completion in the world and in the here and now, and it is based on false premises and assumptions about yourself and the world.

You will not be able to change this narrative by imposing a different set of thoughts and ideas on top of the false ones. There is no qualitative difference in our thoughts; a "noble" thought is no different from a "carnal" thought.

Instead, you are going to observe and record, as you have done for more than two weeks now. However, in order to unthread your narrative, you have to use dynamic observing. Dynamic observing, as we saw yesterday, uses open questions and waits in silence and stillness for a response.

Patience is the key to this exercise. You are the attentive angler waiting on the riverbank for a pull on your fishing line. Most thoughts you have are inconsequential mutterings that roll across your mind. These you should observe and record in the same manner that you have been doing for more than two weeks now.

What you are waiting for in this exercise is a thought sequence based on a supportive narrative. Although no more significant than your random thoughts, the supportive-narrative thoughts will seem to be more substantial or important. They will have a sense of urgency, necessity, or a goal to be reached. Examples include: "I must do this because. . . " or: "If I can get this done, I'll. . . ". Both require underlying assumptions of a world from which you are utterly separate, in which effort is needed in order to succeed, and where a cause always produces a predictable effect. Another example referred to several times in this program is: "If I observe my thoughts long enough, I shall become enlightened." Look closely at the structure of that thought, and you will see a number of assumptions underpinning it. The first and most obvious assumptions to observe are that: a) enlightenment is a state, b) it is a state worth being in, and c) you are not in that state. Furthermore, it includes an assumption of an effort/reward trade-off, based on the age-old belief that you get what you want only from hard work. The most fundamental assumption of all, of course, is that there is a fixed "I" who will benefit from this state of enlightenment.

Each of these assumptions needs to be examined, but you do not have to go through a rigorous intellectual exercise in order to do so. The watchful waiting of dynamic observing will unstitch your story. Your assumptions and your narrative about them are not explicit; they are part of a mass hypnosis that has affected all of us. None of us questions who we are and the world we inhabit; instead, it is as if we have all agreed amongst ourselves about how it must be and how we will live in the world.

So, questions that have a sense of necessity or urgency, or a result in mind, will lead you to your tacit assumptions. Regard them as nothing more substantial than a "pyramid of smoke." Nevertheless, to continue the metaphor, smoke gets in your eyes and eventually becomes all you are able to see.

As is usually the case, you may be unconscious when you have these thoughts – in fact, by now you probably realize that thoughts from the Past time-body happen only when you are unconscious. The important thing about unthreading your story is to exercise the muscle of awareness after the fact and quietly pull apart the thought. Let us say, as an example, that your special thought was something like, "I must get this finished so that I can get home." That kind of thought requires a number of concepts and associations. There has to be a correlation between the finishing of the task and your ability to leave the office, an association between finishing and reward, a concept of "work place" and "home."

There is nothing wrong with any of these thoughts, any more than there is with any other thought pattern. The exercise requires you merely to observe them and their underlying assumptions. You do not change anything, you do not beat yourself up over the thought – that would be a different movement of thought: you merely observe without judgment or desire to change.

The point is to take you deeper and to make you more conscious, like moving up to a more advanced class at the gym; you are ready for a slightly tougher workout. That is its sole purpose. While you are conscious, while you are the attentive angler sitting expectantly on the riverbank, you will not have those thoughts – or any thoughts at all.

When you are unconscious, the Past time-body will dominate. As with the other exercises in the *Time-Light* program, unthreading your story will help you strengthen the focus of the Potential center.

Day 20 ▶ The healing begins

Yet another exercise – and by now you probably do need six pages per day. Copy across all the sections from Day 19 and add the new section: "The healing begins." Still wearing that piece of string?

After publishing a health journal for more than twenty years, I am staggered by how many people suffer from some illness, many of them chronic, often life-threatening, and almost all debilitating to some degree. For many reasons, there are far too many people walking around with a health challenge that they just put up with. Even if you are physically well, you may carry around some psychological problems – trauma, depression, anxiety, or worse.

Why is there so much sickness in the world when, after millions of years of evolution, we should enjoy almost perpetual health? We now know we have Three Selves, or energy centers, and that each has to work with the others if we are to be whole and free of disease. The Present time-body has to satisfy its needs without the unconscious interference of the Past time-body, which constantly subverts its desire for good, healthy nutrition for "reward" food and drink. The Past time-body has to become a conscious movement. The Potential center must be acknowledged and allowed to manifest through us and into the world.

There are two possible causes of disease: those that happen in time and space, and those that happen outside of both. I do not believe these are two distinct groupings; there is a complex interplay between the two. A disease that originates outside of time and space may be amplified within the two other dimensions. An example of this is a person who gives up the will to live, and loses his energy for life. While we live in the Present, this phenomenon could not happen because we would be simple enough to live from moment to moment. However, because of the patterning from the Past, we are complex beings and cannot see the simplicity of life and that which is in front of us. As a result, life can become too much, and we lose the will to live.

Another example of this complex of time-states is in a person who continues to smoke when he is fully aware of the enormous damage he is likely to be causing. Although a smoker is chemically addicted, an incident in time and space, the continuing motivation to smoke is taking place beyond either.

The first causes of illness – reactions that occur entirely in time and space – are well recorded, and are the stuff of medicine and biology. For example, someone becomes ill following poisoning from pollutants, such as pesticides, is injured following an accident, or reacts to a pharmaceutical drug. Time-and-space-related illnesses that may have some crossover with causes outside of these dimensions include poor diets, poor general lifestyle, hereditary issues, and contagion. Cancer, for example, can be a disease entirely developed in time and space, such as when it is caused by exposure to toxic chemicals. It can be a crossover illness involving some morbid influence from the Past time-body. But cancer can also be the result of a diminishing of the will to live, which occurs when pulses from the Past completely overshadow the Potential center. This can happen for a number of reasons, but when we just do not see the point of living anymore, we are separated from the Potential, a center that becomes opaque if we are completely in the thrall of the Past time-body.

Illness can be entirely caused by the Past time-body, resulting from such thoughts such as "I told you so," "Look what you have done to me," and "I deserve this because I'm worthless/ugly /disappointing, etc."

Psychological problems are invariably emotional. Nevertheless, it is also important to consider the Present time-body as a possible influence, since allergies and chemical reactions play a big part in depressive and other so-called mental illness. These kinds of conditions also occur when the Potential center is completely shut off, and we lose all sense of purpose or values.

So what to do? Using your Work Book, write down any health or psychological challenge you have right now. It may be something obvious such as arthritis, or not so apparent, such as a deep-seated emotional issue about your worth or place in the world. It is important to be still when performing this exercise. The exercises so far described should be giving you a fair degree of practice in stillness in your day-to-day life by now.

After you have described your health challenge, I want you to be very honest as you now write down from where you think it originates. It may be relatively straightforward, at the physical, time-and-space level, in which case it derives from the Present time-body. For most of you, it will also involve the Past time-body to a greater or lesser extent, and this too should be recorded. If you have deep depression and you are at your wit's end, or you cannot see the point of living, then you have lost sight of the Potential center, and you need to write that down, too.

If your health issue is entirely at the level of the Present time-body, the remedy is relatively simple: stop or get away from that which is causing it. Many health problems are caused by a poor diet and consumption of processed "white" foods, so look to clean up your act. If it is a crossover problem, you need to examine both your lifestyle and your Past time-body – work that is ongoing in this program.

If your health problem is a crossover it is made up of more than one time-body; if it is entirely emotional, emanating from the Past time-body, the earlier exercises on forgiveness and gratitude are especially helpful. Forgive with your heart anyone who has hurt you and whose hurt you continue to bear; be grateful for the life you have — indeed that you are alive at all.

If you have truly lost sight of the Potential center, forgiveness and gratitude are also important exercises, as are affirmations. These are positive statements about yourself and the world, such as "The world is a friendly place," or "I deserve all the good things that the world has for me." You need to change your tapes consciously, and quickly. This also has the effect of stilling the Past time-body, which will allow the Potential center to rise naturally.

From stillness comes great joy, the beginning of a healing that will last a lifetime.

Day 21 ▶ Service: The New Imitation

So we come to the final lesson on the last day: service. Service to others, in subtle and explicit ways, is selflessness in action. It says that others come before me, because I am nothing but an expression of the unified field, as they are, too. Copy across all the sections from Day 20, and add a new page, with the word "Service" at the top.

Service lies at the heart of the spiritual life (and by "spiritual", I mean the extent to which the Potential center is allowed to express itself). The Potential center is the field of unity and ultimately your true state of being, to which you will eventually return.

The point of life is really to see that you are that and to discover to what extent you can express the Potential center in the Present center of time and space. How much unity, or love, can you bring into the world of seeming separation?

As we have seen throughout this book, the sense of a separate self grows as we become more time-heavy. It is demonstrated in a wide spectrum of ways: a sense of hatred of the world, cynicism, spite, anger, disappointment, depression, weariness, conceit, or, in my case, a sense of pride.

All of these patterns separate you from the feeling of unity and your true inheritance. The miracle of realizing that you are infinite and eternal whilst living in time and space is denied you.

Service that is carried out consciously is a bridge between the sense of a separate self and the Potential center. It can be the smallest act – such as letting someone go before you in a line – or something so large and magnificent that it becomes the stuff of headline news, such as feeding starving children.

What you actually do in service is secondary to the act itself, because the small and the grand action are saying the same thing:

I am not separate, but an expression of a unified field.

If you are proud or conceited, as I was, it is very hard initially to respond to any experience without seeing yourself first. A proud or conceited person always thinks, "How does this affect me?" before any other thought. For me, this sense of pride was a mirror pattern that increased in energy over the years from the initial experiences of an abusive father who consistently told me that I was inadequate and second best.

So, from Day 21, I want you to do something that is in service to others. It may start small – try opening the door for someone – the expression can grow as you volunteer to work in a soup kitchen or help feed the destitute in your neighborhood. Whatever the act, say this to yourself as you do it: "I do this in service to you, a fellow expression of the unified field."

In the 15th century, Thomas a Kempis wrote the classic work of Christian literature, *The Imitation of Christ*. Kempis outlines how, by imitating the selfless acts of Christ, we can attain Christhood (or enlightenment) in this life. The Gospels represent one of the finest expressions of selflessness and love. As love is the continual sense of unity, so its expression is the selfless act. Day 21 is, therefore, the New Imitation.

You may be wondering how it could be that, in a twenty-one-day program, we should be starting a new lesson today. Surely, such an important act as service should not be relegated to merely one day? Of course not, and that is because the program is a continual loop that you repeat until you "get it." Thereafter, you do not need it anymore. Just as the child learns to write in a straight line by following the lines on a piece of paper, so you will grow beyond the program and the model of the Three Selves, and into the continual now of eternity and selfhood.

Afterword

Most therapies try to deal head-on with a problem from the past. Not only is this impossible, it is also unnecessary. Instead, the *Time-Light* program deals with the energetic processes – and the process is the same for each experience that has been partially understood or witnessed.

Many of you may be wondering why, through the entire program, I have not once spoken about meditation or, come to that, God. In fact, I have been writing about nothing else. All of the exercises achieve the aim of meditation – of stilling "the mind," or, more precisely, the Past time-body. As that becomes more still, so the Potential self, the center that allows you to fall back in love with your life, can rise.

Enlightenment, fulfilment, a love of life – none of these is achieved by gaining things, but by letting things go. The main thing you have to let go of is the Past time-body, the unconscious shadow that blocks out the Potential center. While you are living in the past and through time, you cannot be present, and the Potential is apparent only in the now.

There is certainly nothing wrong with meditating, but some people do it for a purpose: They think that by being still they will be rewarded by becoming blissfully happy or enlightened. All of this is an attempt to move from unhappiness and to an imagined state of non-unhappiness. It is part of the same process that gets the banker up every morning: If I do this, I will get that.

Instead, my approach is meditation by stealth. I offer no reward or prize when you carry out the simple exercises of observing, recording, and vocalizing. There can be no reward because "you" are the prize you seek, but one of your time-bodies dominates and masks that truth. Any movement away from "you" takes you further from the prize, which is you.

So, instead of encouraging movement – do this to get that – I encourage stillness, a natural consequence of observing and recording. When the Past time-body is observed, when "you" are present, its unconscious behavior patterns are frozen. "You" have to become unconscious, or lose conscious awareness of the Past time-body, in order for it to function. And when it does, the whole mirage of personal narrative, the pyramid of smoke, the past living through time – all of this begins to rise up, creating your world and a "you" in it.

The aim of this program is for you to fall back in love with your life. You have fallen out of love by going out into the world in search of happiness and in search of a self that you believe is lost. Past trauma, unhappiness and disappointment has caused a disconnection within yourself so that the Three Selves have operated independently, utterly unaware of the others. A love of life is found only by living in the here and now. Most of us live in and through time, and in so doing, we fail to meet the challenge of the vibrant and ever-changing now. The only way you connect with the now is by living in the now, and not by being burdened down by the past, forever interpreting the now through the filters of yesterday.

The key is that there is no "how" to get to the present; any formula consists of the past, a dead format. While carrying out the 21-day program, you may have noticed that while you are observing, there is nothing to record – because there are no thoughts rising up from the Past time-body.

There is much talk and speculation about the nature of enlightenment and love. In fact, they are the same thing. Love is a complete knowing that everything is unified, which is the true state of the Potential center. It is also knowing that there is no separate and substantial "I" that exists independently of the world. Religions have all sorts of different words for love; the Indian religions call it Nirvana, and the Christians call it heaven. Its opposite is not hate, but the sense of a lack of love. Hell is the sense of disunity and separateness. There is nothing more hellish than feeling utterly alone, helpless, and separate.

If we are unconscious, we are living to some degree in hell. The poor souls who are suicidal are at the far edge of a sense of extreme separation and can see no way out of their despair of utter aloneness. The urge to commit suicide is also an indication of the extent of your blindness to the Potential center in you. A realized or enlightened person knows that he is the Potential, that there is no division in life, and that we are all one. Truly knowing this is a coming home, a return to Eden, a falling back in love with your life.

Your path has taken you to this book and to this point, and there is no going back. Now the path disappears; it has no beginning or end, no destination, no reward. It is a continual loop of awareness. And so, with pencil in hand, I invite you to start with me again from Day 1 and into eternity.

GLOSSARY

In creating the philosophy of the Three Selves and the Time-Light program, I have invented some new terms or used existing terms in slightly different ways. Here is a glossary of these terms for ready reference. "Cf" placed beside any other term in an entry means "see also" that definition for further clarification.

Addictive behavior patterns: Most of us have addictions, whether to drink, food, sex, or shopping. These are repetitive behaviors based on experiences. They arise from the Past time-body, specifically the Psychological self (cf), and they are an attempt to rekindle a past sense of oneness or completeness, but result from a wrong association. If, for example, you had a sense of completeness while holding a glass of wine, you might wrongly identify that sense with alcohol, and so seek to experience it again through drink. Ironically, any strengthening of the Past time-body through addictive behavior reduces those moments of unity (which arise from the Potential center (cf)). Ultimately, any movement from the Past time-body seeks completion through understanding. Seen that way, an addiction is a pattern that seeks completion and an end. It comes from ecstasy, joy, and a sense of unity – not from sadness. Some addictions do have a biochemical component, and it is important to tackle these within the Present time-body.

Animal self: This is another term for the Present time-body. It encompasses the body and brain and the world in time and space. The animal self has its own needs and its emotions, but they are related to the here and now.

Associated addictions: Most of the addictions I discuss are associated addictions. They come about when an oceanic feeling of love or unity occurs while you were doing something else. That something else, such as drinking a glass of wine or driving a sports car, becomes the object or action associated with the feeling, and so you seek to repeat it. (cf: psychological witchcraft)

Changing the tape: A technique in which you consciously change thought patterns. Most of us have a pattern in our life – a difficulty holding down a job, say, or saving money – based on a pattern of thought, of which we are unaware, that helps to create our reality. These thoughts, in turn, are based on a series of assumptions, which, when examined, are arrived at from surprisingly little information, often just a few experiences. All these patterns begin as a pulse from the Psychological Past (cf).

Clear experiences: A clear experience is one that leaves no energetic footprint; it is a full experience in the moment. Very few of us have clear experiences. Most of us have partial experiences, usually based on our own limited point of view and seen through the eyes of our own Past time-body. A partial experience leaves an energetic print in the Past time-body and will continue to rise up through the Present time-body in order to complete the experience.

Commander Self: The Commander Self is one of the greatest fictions that affect humanity. It is the sense that there is a "real" you, which is consistent and enduring, that controls all thoughts and emotions. The belief in a Commander Self is at the heart of many therapies, which suggests that "you" – a Commander Self – suppresses unpleasant thoughts and places them into a subconscious. This same "you" can dscover these thoughts and work on them.

Direct addiction: Unlike an associated addiction (cf), a direct addiction is one in which someone takes a drug, such as LSD, specifically to create an oceanic feeling. For this form of addiction to end, the addict needs to experience the feeling of love and unity naturally.

Displaced concept: Impulses from the Past time-body (cf) seek final understanding and resolution of an experience that was not completely understood. It does so only through the Present time-body (cf) within time and space. However, this is a futile endeavor as the original situation and characters have changed or have died. The best the conceptual brain can do is to create either a pattern, so that the experience is repeated as closely as possible to the original situation, or a displaced concept, where a sense of loss may be transferred to a different person or situation.

Dynamic observing: Most of us sleepwalk through our lives. We are barely conscious of our own thoughts or the world around us. Dynamic observing is a way of being sensitive to every influence and seeing yourself in the experience, too. It also involves asking yourself open questions, and feeling the responses, rather than intellectualizing them. Often, the closest we get to a dynamic observation is when we are suddenly embarrassed. At that moment, we clearly see others and ourselves.

Emotions: It is natural to have emotions. All Three Selves trigger emotions: The Present self has immediate emotions related to the world in time and space, such as fear, anger, kindness, grief and generosity, while the highest emotion of the Past self is empathy. The Past time-body is also the store of past emotions related to previous experiences, and these are replayed in the Present. Only the Potential center expresses true love, a sense of unity with all things.

EsTS: Events outside of time and space (cf).

Events outside of time and space: Although we appear to live in a world of time and space, governed by natural laws, we all occasionally have experiences that seem to contradict these physical laws. We experience this at a mundane level whenever we get a phone call from someone we have been thinking about or become aware of people staring at the back of our head. Countless instances of telepathy, clairvoyance, near-death experiences and premonitions have been recorded, and a good number scientifically verified. I call these experiences Events outside of Time and Space (EsTS).

Facts: The world is made up of facts. It is a fact that there is a war, it is a fact that I am in debt, it is a fact that my car has broken down. We give these facts meaning by investing them with values and emotions. We accentuate facts and often make any situation worse by becoming emotional about them. This also prevents us from acting coherently to improve the existing situation. As the world is made up only of facts, we can do just two things in the world: act, if it is within our power to do so or do nothing.

Forgiveness: Forgiveness is for your own benefit, not for the person you are forgiving. It is a letting go of a past energetic imprint. Letting go and forgiveness are the natural consequences of fully understanding a situation. Only when you fully understand an experience by using dynamic observing (cf) will you naturally forgive and so let go. Dynamic observing occurs at a point of great stillness, when all three time-bodies are coordinated. You are then fully conscious.

Fully witnessed: A fully witnessed experience takes account of the complete situation, its origins, and the characters involved, including their motivation. In that instance, a situation is fully understood, and is complete. As such, it does not seek reiteration in the Present time-body (cf) in order to find complete understanding and resolution. An experience that is fully witnessed leaves no energetic trace in the Past time-body (cf).

Genius: The prevailing view is that genius is a quality of the brain, and is the next logical step on from being extremely intelligent. This is not always the case: a genius from the world of the arts, for example, may have an average intelligence. According to the Three Selves model, genius is the degree to which someone is sensitive to his or her Potential center (cf). Most moments of special inspiration happen in a way that the person cannot account for it. An insight seems to happen "out of the blue"; in fact, it occurs outside of space and time, and enters the world through the recipient's brain. The brain is therefore merely the receiver of inspirational pulses from the Potential center, and a genius has a brain that is "tuned in" at an appropriate moment.

Hannah filter: Hannah was the name of Isaac Newton's mother. It is a palindrome – it reads the same backward or forward.

Newton proved that white light is made up of a spectrum of colors, from the one to the many. I have used it as a metaphor for the Three Selves that arise from the Potential center, the field of being. Ultimately, the three return to the one (just as, in reverse, a spectrum of colors can be turned into white light).

Hungry mind: This occurs when the Present combines with the Psychological past to create an energy pattern that suggests the next new thing – be it a car, a book, or a house – will make you forever happy, or provide the missing key. It can also be an element of addictive behavior (cf).

I am a camera: This term, coined by the writer Christopher Isherwood, refers to a technique of seeing the world without defining.

Knowledge past: This is an important self from the Past, where skills and expertise, such as fixing a door or changing a tire, live. It is the self that allows us to operate in the world.

Mega-feelings: The Past time-body is made up of partially understood experiences that pulse into the Present time-body, where they become a thought or feeling through the conceptual mind. We rarely define or challenge these feelings, but instead assume that they somehow inform us about reality and the world out there. Mega-feelings are the collective feelings that feed our unquestioned assumptions about the world, such as that I am somehow permanent and substantial, and that there is a world out there, which is separate from my body.

Mirror patterns: Either you repeat the patterns from your past or you react against them — in which case they become mirror patterns. In either case, you are acting unconsciously from the past. A mirror pattern is the exact opposite of your own experience. A woman who was not allowed to go to ballet class as a child, will push her own daughter into attending.

Narrative past: This layer of the Past time-body is the story of "you," and it defines who you are in the world. On its own, the Narrative past is inocuous, but when fused with the Psychological past (cf), it can become volatile. This combination of past selves lies at the root of most wars and strife, which are fueled by a sense of difference, whether in nationality, creed or religion, and by a sense of injustice or wrong from the Psychological past.

Nostos: A Greek word for coming home. Nostos is the ultimate aim of life, but it is achieved only by the conscious person – someone who fully understands with no trace of a Psychological past in the Past time-body (the Narrative and Knowledge past selves survive this process). Home is the Potential center arising naturally in the Present time-body, and the gate that bars entry is the Psychological self. Nostos, or home-coming, occurs when this Psychological self comes to know itself. This process has been illustrated in different cultures and religions throughout the ages, from the banishment from the Garden of Eden to the homecoming of Odysseus.

Past time-body: One of the Three Selves, the Past is the accumulation of all experience. It comprises three sub-selves: the Narrative, the Knowledge and the Psychological selves. It sits between the Present and Potential selves, and although it exists outside of time and space, it invariably identifies with the Present as it seeks to relive partially observed experiences. However, it is also aware of the infinity of the Potential. This creates a tension, a yearning in the Present that is never satisfied. The highest expression of the past time-body is empathy.

Potential center: One of the Three Selves, the Potential is the ground of being and the field of all possibility. Although the primary source for life, it sits outside of space and time. The Potential is a unified field that seeks to know itself through the relative reality of separation and multiplicity of life. Depending on the culture, it is also known as consciousness, Atman, God, Mind, the Christ, the Buddha, and the Father.

Present time-body: The one self that exists in its own creation of influences from the world. Because the Present is the only self that is palpable, it becomes diseased from direct causes in the environment and from emotions trapped in the Past self.

Psychological past: One of the three sub-selves in the Past time-body, this is the center for all experience that is not fully comprehended or observed. As all of life is a movement towards greater understanding, so the Psychological past seeks to reenact these experiences through the Present time-body in order to reach completion with full understanding. It is the one barrier between you and enlightenment, but a necessary one as it enables you to become conscious.

Psychological witchcraft: This occurs as the result of an ecstatic moment. As we wish to repeat and understand it, we attempt to recreate the same situation as when we had the original experience in order to invite back the feeling that occurred at the time. This is a form of witchcraft and the root of addictive behaviour.

Pulses: The Three Selves are energy patterns; as such, they communicate by means of pulses or waves, which are immediately interpreted by the brain in the Present time-body as thoughts, emotions, and concepts. An energetic pulse precedes every thought and emotion.

Reacting: Most of us react to a challenge in the Present. This invariably involves a blind or involuntary lashing out because it is a pattern we already recognize. If an experience is completely new — which becomes increasingly unlikely as we age — we do not have a referencing pattern and so instead simply respond (cf).

The Recorder: We live internal lives. Our thoughts become like giants to us and take on enormous significance. The Recorder can be either another person or a voice recorder, to whom (or which) we talk about our thoughts, especially as we have recorded them in our Work Book. The Recorder is no more or less than a set of ears, who listens without comment, reassurance, understanding, or any communication other than the acknowledgment that he or she has heard you.

Responding: This is the appropriate way to meet any experience and challenge. It is measured and conscious and, as such, defuses a tense or angry situation. To respond requires us to see the situation as utterly new and unique, for which we have no preceding pattern. In theory, every experience in the Present is new — by definition that must be so — but usually we react (cf), because it is a pattern we recognize from a past and incomplete experience.

Thought locating: All thoughts begin as a pulse (cf) from one of the Three Selves. As you become more sensitive, you will be able to recognize the source of each of the pulses.

Three Selves: For 3000 years, philosophers and now scientists and neurosurgeons have tried to arrive at a definition of the self and consciousness. Today, the primary theory holds that the sense of self is nothing more than neural firings in the brain between the left and right hemispheres and so a fiction created from the body. However, this interpretation fails to capture the true richness and complexity of the human experience. I believe the sense of "I" is the sum total of pulses from the Three Selves, energetic patterns that I call the Present, the Past (itself made up of three sub-selves), and the Potential, or ground of being. The sense of self is dependent on the dominant pulse at any one time, which is why "you" constantly change. The idea that you are a constant self is a fiction; the only constancy is in the Potential center, and that is impersonal.

Time: Two of the Three Selves produce variations of time: The Present creates and imprints serial time — as we understand the concept of time as something relentlessly moving forward — onto the eternal. The Psychological past creates psychological time. All of thought is a movement of psychological time, from the past to some future, be it moments ahead.

Time-heavy: As we age, we become time-heavy with the burden of experience that still sits as an energetic print in the Psychological past. And as we become more time-heavy through the unconscious pulses from the Psychological Past (cf), we become unhappier and less able to feel any sense of joy.

Time-Light: Most children are *Time-Light* because they have not accumulated experiences that they have not fully understood. When we are *Time-Light*, the dominant pulses emanate from the Present time-body and the Potential center, from where the sense of joy and unity derives. We feel a sense of pleasure from experiences in the Present time-body, but unless these experiences are clear (cf), they will imprint into the Psychological Past time-body and create a pattern of pulses that seek repetition.

Universal subjectivity: We all believe we are having separate and individual experiences, even though we are, in fact, expressions of the same unified field. I call this phenomenon "universal subjectivity" — everyone thinks he or she is separate and having a separate experience within a body, and yet no one actually is.